Little Red Book

of

Idioms and Phrases

By the same author

Treasure Chest for Public Speaking
Read Write Right: Common Errors in English

Little Red Book Series

Little Red Book of SMS Slang-Chat Room Slang
Little Red Book of English Vocabulary
Little Red Book of Grammar Made Easy
Little Red Book of Euphemisms
Little Red Book of English Proverbs
Little Red Book of Acronyms and Abbreviations
Little Red Book of Modern Writing Skills
Little Red Book of Effective Speaking Skills

A2Z Book Series

A2Z Quiz Book
A2Z Book of Word Origins

Others

The Book of Motivation
The Book of Virtues
The Book of Firsts and Lasts
The Book of Fun Facts
The Book of More Fun Facts

Little Red Book
of
Idioms and Phrases

Terry O'Brien

RUPA

Published by
Rupa Publications India Pvt. Ltd 2011
7/16, Ansari Road, Daryaganj
New Delhi 110002

Sales centres:
Allahabad Bengaluru Chennai
Hyderabad Jaipur Kathmandu
Kolkata Mumbai

ISBN: 978-81-291-1811-0

Fourth impression 2015

10 9 8 7 6 5 4

The moral right of the author has been asserted.

Typeset by Innovative Processors, Delhi

Printed at Shree Maitrey Printech Pvt. Ltd., Noida

I dedicate this book to late Prof. A.P. O'Brien,
my father, friend, guide and mentor, who
inspired me to the canon of excellence:
re-imagining what's essential

PREFACE

An idiom is an expression or a phrase whose meaning cannot be easily understood from the individual meanings of the words it contains. Idioms can be defined as expressions which are peculiar to a language. They play an important part in all languages.

The expression 'A bull in a China shop' literally would make one wonder what a bull is doing and that too in a shop when 'China' actually is a city but such an idiomatic expression is peculiar to a language. These are words which when taken together, mean something different from the literal meaning and so is called an idiom.

In an idiom the grammatical construction and the vocabulary used is fixed. If we change them we lose the meaning of the idiom. 'The cat among the pigeons' means 'some troublesome idea or person'. If we change the grammatical construction of this idiom and write it or say it as 'Be careful there is a cat here save the pigeons' then we have actually changed the idiomatic meaning altogether.

In the expression 'throw the towel' one can easily understand the meaning of the various individual words without realizing that the phrase means 'to give in' 'to admit defeat'. This idiom comes from the world of boxing in which 'throwing in the towel' indicates a method of conceding defeat. People use **idioms** to make their language richer and more colourful and to convey subtle shades of meaning or intention. The idiom better describes the full nuance of meaning. Idioms and idiomatic expressions can be more precise than the literal words, often using fewer words but saying more.

Little Red Book of Idioms and Phrases will help you add spice, colour and flavour to your speaking and writing skills. This book has American Idioms and English idioms, all there for the grabs!

Happy reading

Terry O'Brien

American Idioms and Phrases

Able to fog a mirror	Alive, even if just barely (Usually jocular. Refers to the use of a small mirror placed under the nose to tell if a person is breathing or not)
Above par	Better than average or normal
Above the fray	Not involved in a fight or argument; aloof from a fight or argument
Act of faith	An act or deed demonstrating religious faith
Act your age	Behave more maturely
Afraid of own shadow	Easily frightened; always frightened, timid or suspicious
All agog	Surprised and amazed
All and sundry	Everyone; one and all
In the family	Restricted to one's own family or closest friends, as with private or embarrassing information
All over town	In many places in town
All sweetness and light	Very kind, innocent, and helpful
All thumbs	Very awkward and clumsy, especially with one's hands
All walks of life	All social, economic and ethnic groups

All wool and a yard wide	Trustworthy and genuinely good (A description of good quality wool cloth)
Alpha and omega	The essentials, from the beginning to the end; everything, from the beginning to the end
Alphabet soup	Initialisms and acronyms, especially when used excessively
Ambulance chaser	A lawyer who hurries to the scene of an accident to try to get business from injured persons
American as apple pie	Quintessentially American
American dream	Financial stability as well as physical and emotional stability
Answer for	To vouch for someone; to tell the goodness of someone's character
Ants in pants	The imaginary cause of nervousness and agitation
Apple-polisher	A flatterer
Armed to the teeth	Heavily armed with deadly weapons
Article of faith	A statement or element of strong belief
As the crow flies	Straight (route)
Ask for the moon	To make outlandish requests or demands for something, such as a lot of money or special privileges

Asleep at the switch	Not attending one's job; failing to do one's duty at the proper time
Asleep at the wheel	Asleep while behind the steering wheel of a car or other vehicle
At a premium	At a high price; priced high because of something special
At cross purposes	With opposing viewpoints; with goals that interfere with each other
At first blush	When first examined or observed
At loose ends	Restless and unsettled; unemployed
At sixes and sevens	Lost in bewilderment; at loose ends
At the drop of a hat	Immediately on the slightest signal or urging
At the end of the day	At the time when work or one's waking hours end
At the last minute	At the last possible chance; in the last few days, minutes or hours
At the mercy of	Under the control of someone; without defense against someone
Babe in the woods	A naive or innocent person; an experienced person
Back to basics	Return to basic instruction; start the learning process over again
Back to the drawing board	Time to start from the start; it is time to plan something over again
Back to the salt mines	Time to return to work, school, or something else that might be unpleasant

Backfire on	To fail unexpectedly; to fail with a desired result
Backseat driver	An annoying passenger who tells the driver how to drive; someone who tells others how to do things
Bad hair day	Bad day in general
Bag of bones	An extremely skinny person or animal with bones showing
Ball park figure	An estimate; an off-the-cuff guess
Baptism of fire	A first experience of something, usually something difficult or unpleasant
Bargaining chip	Something to be used (traded) in negotiations
Bark up the wrong tree	To make the wrong choice; to ask the wrong person; to follow the wrong course
Battle of the bulge	The attempt to keep one's waistline slim
Battle royal	A classic, hard fought battle or argument
Beat one's gums	To waste time talking a great deal without results
Beat the clock	To do something before a deadline; to finish before the time is up
Begin to see daylight	To begin to see the end of a task
Behind bars	In jail

Belabor the point	To spend too much time on one item
Belt the grape	To drink wine or liquor heavily and become intoxicated
Beyond ken	Outside the extent of one's knowledge
Best bib and tucker	One's best clothing
Beyond one's ken	Outside the extent of one's knowledge or understanding
Big frog in the small pond	An important person amidst less important people
Big apple	New York city
Binge and purge	To overeat and vomit, alternatively and repeatedly
Blank check	Freedom or permission to act as one wishes or thinks necessary
Body politic	The people of a country or state considered as a political unit
Booby prize	A mock prize given to the worst player or performer
Bow and scrape	To be very humble and subservient
Break a story	To be the first to broadcast or distribute the story of an event
Break out into a cold sweat	To become frightened or anxious and begin to sweat
Break the bank	To use up all one's money

Bright-eyed and bushy tailed	Awake and alert
Broken dreams	Wishes or desires that cannot be fulfilled
Build a better mouse-trap	To develop or invent something superior to a device that is widely used
Bum steer	Misleading instructions or guidance; a misleading suggestion
Bumper to bumper	Close together and moving slowly
Burned to a cinder	Burned very badly
Burst bubble	To destroy someone's illusion or delusion; to destroy someone's fantasy
Butterflies in one's stomach	A nervous feeling in one's stomach
By shank's mare	By foot; by walking
Can of worms	A very difficult issue or set of problems; an array of difficulties
Can't carry a tune in a paper sack	Unable to sing or hum a melody
Can't carry a tune in a bucket	Same as "can't carry a tune in a paper sack"
Can't hit the (broad) side of a barn	Cannot aim something accurately

Can't unring the bell	Cannot undo what's been done
Carve out a niche	To have developed and mastered one's own special skill
Cause some tongues to wag	To cause people to gossip
Catch-as-catch-can	The best one can do with whatever is available
Chapter and verse	Very specifically detailed, in reference to sources of information
Cheap at half the price	Nicely priced; fairly valued; bargain priced
Chew one's cud	To think deeply
Chin music	Talk; conversation
Chunk of change	A lot of money
Cloak-and-dagger	Involving secrecy and plotting
Close as two coats of paint	Close and intimate
Come a cropper	To have misfortune; to fail
Come unglued	To lose emotional control; to break out into tears of laughter
Compare apples and oranges	To compare two entities that are not similar
Cook one's goose	To damage or ruin someone
Cow juice	Milk

Crack under the strain	To have a mental or emotional collapse because of stress or continued work
Cream of the crop	The best of all
Creature comforts	Things that make people comfortable
Cut corners	To take short-cuts; to save money or effort by finding cheaper or easier ways to do something
Dead from the neck up	Stupid
Diamond in the rough	A person who has good qualities despite a rough exterior; a person with great potential
Disaster of epic proportions	A very large disaster
Do damnedest	To do as well as one can, not sparing any energy or determination
Do the honors	To act as hostess and serve one's guests
Doggy bag	A bag or container to carry uneaten food home from a restaurant
Dog and pony show	Display, demonstration or exhibition of something- such as something one might be selling
Dollar for dollar	Considering the amount of money involved; considering the cost of value
Done by/with mirrors	Illusory; purposefully deceptive

Drag feet	To progress slowly or stall in the doing of something
Drawn and quartered	To be dealt with severely
Drop like flies	To faint, sicken, collapse or die in great numbers like houseflies dying in a large group
Duck and cover	To bend down and seek protection against an attack
Dyed-in-the-wool	Permanent or extreme
Eager-beaver	Someone who is very enthusiastic, someone who works very hard
Early bird	A person who gets up early
Easy does it	Move slowly and carefully
Eat one's heart out	To grieve; to be sorrowful
Eat like a bird	To eat small portions of food; to peck at one's food
Even steven	To be even (with someone or something) by having repaid a debt, relied in kind, etc.
Every nook and cranny	Every small, out-of-the-way place or places where something can be hidden
Every trick in the book	Every deceptive method known
Eyeball to eyeball	Face-to-face and often very close; in person

Fall between two stools	To come somewhere between the two possibilities and so fail to meet the requirements of either
Fancy footwork	Clever and intricate dance steps
Fancy meeting you here	I am very surprised to meet you here!
Fat and sassy	In good health and spirits
Feel blue	To feel sad
Fifth wheel	An extra or unwelcomed person
Fine and dandy	Fine; good; well
Fish for a compliment	Try to get someone to pay oneself a compliment
Fish tale	Great big lie
Flex muscles	To do something that shows potential, strength, power, or ability
Flirt with disaster	To take great risks; to tempt fate
Float a loan	To get a loan of money; to arrange for a loan of money
For the birds	Worthless; undesirable
Forty winks	A nap; some sleep
Frog in one's throat	A feeling of hoarseness or a lump in one's throat
From scratch	By starting with the basic ingredients (making something)
Fudge factor	A margin of error
Full of holes	Cannot stand up to challenge or scrutiny (of an argument or plan)

Funny ha-ha	Amusing; comical
Funny peculiar	Odd; eccentric
Gales of laughter	Repeated choruses of laughter
Get down to business/work	To begin to get serious; to begin to negotiate or conduct business
Get down to the nuts and bolts	To get down to basic facts
Get one's fingers burned	To receive harm or punishment for one's actions
Get one's foot in the door	To complete the first step in a process
Get off the dime	To start moving; to get out of a stopped position
Ghost of a chance	Even the slightest chance
Give a red face	To make someone visibly embarrassed
Give it a rest	Stop talking so much. Give your mouth a rest
Give me a break	Don't be so harsh on me; give me another chance
Give up the ghost	To die
Glutton for punishment	Someone willing to accept difficulty
Gloom and doom	Unpleasant predictions, statements or atmospheres

Go fifty-fifty	To divide the cost of something in half with someone
Go haywire	To go wrong; to beak down
Go home in a box	To be shipped home dead
Go over like a lead balloon	To fail completely
Go stag	To go to an event (which is meant for couples) without a member of the opposite sex
Go to hell in a bucket	To get rapidly worse and worse
Go to town	To work hard or very effectively
Go under the knife	To submit to surgery; to have surgery done on oneself
Go whole hog	To do everything possible; to be extravagant
Going great guns	Going fast or energetically
Gone with the wind	Gone as if taken away by the wind
Good riddance (to bad rubbish)	Good to be rid of worthless persons or things
Grandfather Clause	A clause in an agreement that protects certain rights granted in the past even when conditions change in the future
Great balls of fire	Good heavens!; Wow!

Grim reaper	Death
Gut feeling	A personal, intuitive feeling or response
Hail a cab	To signal to a taxi that you want to be picked up
Half a loaf	Small or incomplete portion of something
Hand over fist	Very rapidly (for money and merchandise to be exchanged)
Hang in there	Be patient, things will work out
Hang tough	To stick to one's position
Happy camper	A happy person
Hatchet man	A man who does the cruel or difficult things for someone
Have a bone to pick(with)	To have something to argue about with someone
Have a field day	To experience freedom from one's usual work schedule; to have a very enjoyable time
Have a green thumb	To have the ability to grow plants well
Have a hollow leg	To have a great capacity or need for food or drink, usually the latter
Have a roving eye	To be flirtatious
Have a sweet tooth	To desire to eat many sweet foods- especially candy and pastries
Have a whale of a time	To have an exciting or fun time; to have a big time

Have dibs on	To reserve something for oneself; to claim something for oneself
Have egg on one's face	To be embarrassed by something one has done
Have eyes in the back of one's head	To seem to be able to sense what is going on behind or outside of one's field of vision
Have one's finger in too many pies	To be involved in too many things; to have too many tasks going to be able to do any of them well
Have one's mind in the gutter	Tending to think of or say things that are obscene
Have one's head in the clouds	To daydream
Have kittens	To get extremely upset
Have one's nose in a book	To read books all the time
Have one in the oven	To be pregnant with a child
Have sticky fingers	To have a tendency to steal
Heads will roll	People will get into trouble
Hem and haw (around)	To be uncertain about something; to be evasive; to say "ah" and "eh" when speaking – avoid saying something meaningful
Hidden agenda	A secret plan; a concealed plan; a plan disguised as a plan with another purpose

Highways and byways	Major and minor roads
Hit the jackpot	To win a large amount of money gambling or in a lottery
Hive of activity	A location where things are very busy
Hold one's liquor	To be able to drink alcohol in quantity without ill-effects
Hold one's tongue	To refrain from speaking; to refrain from saying something unpleasant
Honeymoon is over	The early pleasant beginning (as at the start of a marriage) has ended
Hop, skip and a jump	A short distance
Hot under the collar	Very angry
Hum with activity	To busy with activity (for a place)
Hunt-and-peck	A slow 'system' of typing where one searches for a certain key and then presses it
Hush money	Money paid as a bribe to persuade someone to remain silent and not reveal certain information
Hustle and bustle	Confusion and business
I could eat a horse!	I am very hungry!

I wouldn't touch it with a ten-foot pole	I would not have anything to do with it under any circumstances
Icing on the cake	An extra enhancement
I'll be a monkey's uncle!	I am amazed!
I'll eat my hat	I will be very surprised
In a (pretty) pickle	In a mess; in trouble
In a rut	In a type of boring habitual behavior
In a stew	Upset or bothered about someone or something
In crosshairs	On one's agenda for immediate action; being studied for action at this moment
In dribs and drabs	In small proportions; bit by bit
In hog heaven	Very happy; having a wonderful time
In mint condition	In perfect condition
In stitches	Laughing very hard
In the ballpark	Within prescribed limits; within the anticipated range of possibilities
In the boondocks	In a rural area; far away from a city or population
In the prime of one's life	In the best and most productive and healthy period of life

In tune with	In agreement with someone or something
In two shakes of a lamb's tail	In a very short time
In and outs (of)	The special things that one needs to know to do something
Inkling (about)	An idea someone or something; a hint about the nature of someone or something
It cuts two ways	There are two sides to the situation
It's a jungle out there	The real world is severe; it's hard to get by in everyday life
It's high time	It is about the right time for something
It's written all over (one's) face	It is very evident and can easily be detected when looking at someone's face
It's you!	It suits you perfectly; it is just your style
It's your funeral	If that is what you're going to do, you will have to endure the dire consequences
Jekyll and Hyde	Someone with both an evil and a good personality
Jog memory	To stimulate someone's memory to recall something
Join the club!	An expression indicating that the person spoken to is in the same, or a similar, unfortunate state as the speaker

Jump the gun	To start before the starting signal (Originally used in sports contests that are started by firing a gun)
Just one's cup of a tea	To be something that one prefers or desires
Just the ticket	To be just the perfect thing
Just what the doctor ordered	Exactly what is required, especially for health or comfort
Kangaroo court	A bogus or illegal court
Katie bar the door	Prepare immediately for an advancing threat
Keep a civil tongue	To speak decently and politely
Keep banker's hours	To work or to be open for business for less than eight hours a day
Keep in there!	Keep trying!
Keep late hours	To stay up or stay out until late at night
Keep one posted	To keep someone informed
Keep the shirt on	To be patient
Keep the wolf from the door	To maintain oneself at a minimal level; to keep from starving, freezing, etc.
Keep your chin up	An expression of encouragement to someone who has to bear some emotional burdens
Kick in the guts	A severe blow to one's body or spirit

Kill the fatted calf	To prepare an elaborate banquet (in someone's honour)
King's ransom	A great deal of money
Kissing cousins	Relatives who know one another well enough to kiss when they meet
Knight in shining armor	A person, usually male, who rescues or assists a person in need of help
Knock-down-drag-out fight	A serious fight; a serious argument
Knuckle sandwich	A punch in the face
Lame duck	Someone who's in the last period of a term in an elective office and cannot run for reelection
Land-office business	A large amount of business done in a short period of time
Laugh all the way to the bank	To be very happy about money that has been earned by doing something that other people might think is unfair or that they criticized
Laugh one's head off	To laugh very hard and loudly; as if one's head might come off
Laugh up one's sleep	To laugh secretly; to laugh quietly to oneself
Lay out in lavender	To scold someone severely
Lead the life of Riley	To live in luxury

Lead-pipe cinch	Something very easy to do; something entirely certain to happen
Lean and mean	Fit and ready for hard, efficient work
Leave a bad taste in one's mouth	To leave a bad feeling with someone
Level playing field	A situation that is fair to all; same opportunity
Leave one high and dry	To recede and leave someone untouched
Less is more	Fewer or smaller is better
Let George do it	Let someone else do it; it doesn't matter who
Let the grass grow under one's feet	To do nothing; to stand still
Let one's hair down	To tell one's inner most feelings and secrets
Lie doggo	To remain unrecognized (for a long time)
Life in the fast lane	A very active or possibly risky life
Life of the party	A person who is lively and helps make a party fun and exciting
Like a ton of bricks	Like a great weight or burden
Like two peas in a pod	Very close or intimate

Line one's won pocket	To make money for oneself in a greedy or dishonest fashion
Little bird told me (a)	You do not want to reveal who told you something
Like a three-ring circus	Chaotic; exciting and busy
Live by wits	To survive by being clever
Live out of cans	To eat only canned food
Loaded to bear	Angry
Lock, stock and barrel	Everything
Long in the tooth	Old
Look good on paper	To seem fine in theory, but not perhaps in practice; to appear to be a good plan
Loose lips sink ships	Don't talk carelessly because you don't know who is listening
Low man on the totem pole	The least important or lowest-ranking person of a group
Lower the boom on	To scold or punish someone severely; to crack down on someone
Low-hanging fruit	The easiest thing to get or achieve; an easy profit
Made to order	Made to one's own measurements and on request
Make a killing	To have a great success, especially in making money

Make it snappy!	Hurry up!; move quickly and smartly
Make or break	To bring success or ruin to someone
Make waves	To cause difficulty; to create a stir
Make one's heart sink	To cause one to respond to something by developing an empty feeling inside
Marvel to behold	Someone or something quite exciting or wonderful to see
Mean streak	A tendency for a person to do things that are mean
Meat-and-potatoes	Basic, sturdy and hearty (Often refers to a robust person, usually a man with simple tastes in food and other things)
Meeting of the minds	The establishment of agreement; complete agreement
Mere trifle	A tiny bit; small, unimportant matter; a small amount of money
Middle-of-the-road	Halfway between two extremes, especially political extremes
Might and main	Great physical strength; great force
Miscarriage of justice	A wrong or mistaken decision; especially one made in a court of law
Miss by a mile	To fail to hit something by a great distance; to land wide of the mark
Mists of time	A long time ago
Mix business with pleasure	To combine business discussions or transactions in a social or holiday setting

Moist around the edges	Intoxicated
Monkey suit	A tuxedo
Mopping-up operation	A cleanup operation; the final stages in a project where the loose ends are taken care of
More bark than bite	More threat than actual harm
More the merrier	The more people there are, the happier the situation will be
Morning after (night before)	A hangover; the feelings associated having drunk too much alcohol
Movers and shakers	People who get things done; organizers and managers
Mum's the word	Nothing is to be said about this; don't say anything about this
Name names	To reveal the names of people who have done something wrong
Neither fish nor fowl	Not any recognizable thing
New kid on the block	A child who has just moved towards a certain neighborhood
New York minute	A very short period of time
No great shakes	Someone or something that isn't very good
No such luck	The luck needed for success simply wasn't available

None of your lip!	Shut up!; I don't want to hear anything from you about anything
Nose is in the air	One acts conceited or aloof
Not a dry eye	No one in a place is free from tears or sobbing
Not one's cup of tea	Not one's choice or preference (used to describe an activity one doesn't enjoy)
Not for all the tea in China	Not even if you rewarded me with all the tea in China; not for anything at all
Not know from Adam	Not to know someone by sight at all
Not let the grass grow under feet	Not to stay in one place for a long time; to be always on the move
Not rocket science	Not some very complicated scientific endeavor allegedly beyond most people
Nuts and bolts	The mundane workings of something; the basics of something
Odd man out	An unusual or atypical person or thing
Off on a tangent	To be on a somewhat related or irrelevant course while neglecting the main subject
Off the charts	Record setting; beyond the expected range of measurement
Off the hook	Freed from an obligation

Old as Methuselah	Very old
Old stamping ground	The place where one was raised or where one has spent a lot of time
Old warhorse	A performance piece that is performed often
On a pedestal	Elevated to a position of honor or reverence
On a shoe string	With a very small amount of money
On a silver platter	Using a presentation (of something) that is appropriate for a very formal setting
On a wing and a prayer	To arrive or fly in with one's plane in very bad condition
On second thought	Having given something more thought: having reconsidered something
On the prowl	Looking for someone for sexual purposes
On the same wavelength	Thinking in the same pattern
One sandwich short of picnic	Not very smart, lacking intelligence
One-night stand	A performance lasting only one night
Out of the ballpark	Greater than the amount of money suggested or available
Over a barrel	Out of one's control; in a dilemma

Pardon me for living!	A very indignant response to a criticism or rebuke
Part hair	To come very close to someone
Patter of tiny feet	The sound of young children; having children in the household
Penny-pincher	Someone who objects to spending of every single penny
Perish the thought	Do not even consider thinking of such a (negative) thing
Pet peeve	A frequent annoyance; one's "favorite" or most often encountered annoyance
Plaster hair down	To use water, oil, or cream to dress the hair for combing
Play hardball (with)	To act strong and aggressive about an issue with someone
Plot thickens	Things are becoming more complicated or interesting
Pocket of resistance	A small group of people who resist change or domination
Pull all the stops out	To use everything available; to not hold back
Pull the rug out	To make someone or someone's plans fall through; to upset someone's plans
Punch a clock	To punch a register once arrival or departure on a workplace time clock or other similar record-keeping device on a daily basis

Put one's best foot forward	To act or appear at one's best; to try to make a good impression
Put one's dibs on	To lay a claim to something to announce one's claim to something
Put one's hand to the plow	To get busy; to help out; to start working
Put one's nose to the grindstone	To get busy doing one's work
Put something on the street	To tell something openly; to spread news
Put out (some) feelers on	To arrange to find out about something in an indirect manner
Quality time	Time spent with someone allowing interaction and closeness
Quit while ahead	To stop doing something while one is still successful
Rags to riches	From poverty to wealth; from modesty to elegance
Rant and rave	To shout angrily and wildly about someone or something
Real McCoy	An authentic thing or person
Recharge batteries	To get some refreshing rest
Regular as clockwork	Very regular; completely predictable
Ride the gravy train	To live in easy or luxury
Right in the kisser	Right in the mouth or face

Ring true	To sound or seem true or likely
Rise and shine!	Get out of bed and be lively and energetic!
Room and board	Food to eat and a place to live; the cost of food and lodging
Royal pain	Great annoyance
Rule with a velvet glove	To rule in a very gentle way
Run on all cylinders	To run well and smoothly
Run rampant	To run, develop, or grow out of control
Safe and sound	Unharmed and whole or healthy
Sea change	A major change or transformation
See stars	To seem to see flashing lights after receiving a blow to the head
See the color of money	To verify that someone has money or has enough money
Sell like hotcakes	To be sold very fast
Set the world on fire	To do exciting things that bring fame and glory
Shady deal	A questionable and possibly dishonest deal or transaction
Sign on the dotted line	To indicate one's agreement to something
Sitting pretty	Living in a good situation

Sixty-four-dollar question	The most important question; the question that everyone wants to know the answer to
Slip trolley	To become a little crazy; to lose one's composure
Smack in the face	Something that will humiliate someone, often when it is considered deserved; an insult
Small potatoes	Something or someone insignificant; small fry
Smoke and mirrors	Deception and confusion
Smoking gun	The indisputable sign of guilt
Soft in the head	Stupid; witless
Soft sell	A polite attempt to sell something; a very gentle sales pitch
Spare tire	A thickness in the waist; a roll of fat around one's waist
Spin a yarn	To tell a tale
Spin doctor	Someone who gives a twisted or deviously deceptive version of an event
Spit and polish	Orderliness; ceremonial precision and orderliness
Squawk about	To complain about something
Start from scratch	To start from the very beginning; to start from nothing
Straight from the shoulder	Very direct, without attenuation or embellishment

Stretch legs	To walk around, stretch, and loosen one's leg muscles after sitting or lying down for a time
Surf and turf	Fish and beef; lobster and beef
Swing into high gear	To begin operating at a fast pace; to increase the rate of activity
Take a backseat	To become less important than someone or something else
Take a turn for the better	To start to improve; to start to get well
Take it on the lam	To get out of town; to run away
Take the Fifth (Amendment)	To claim that telling someone something would get the teller in trouble
Take the plunge	To marry someone
Talk a blue streak	To talk very much and very rapidly
Talk in circles	To talk in a confusing or round about manner
Talk turkey	To talk business; to talk frankly
Tan hide	To spank someone
Tap dance like mad	To appear busy continuously; to have to move fast or talk cleverly to distract someone
Tar and feather	To punish or humiliate someone by coating them with tar and feathers
Teething troubles	Pain and crying on the part of a baby whose teeth are growing in

Telegraph punches	To signal, unintentionally, what blows one is about to strike
There are plenty of (other) fish in the sea	There are other choices
Think on feet	To be able to speak and reason well while in front of an audience, especially extemporaneously
Through the cracks	Past the elements that are intended to catch or detect such things (moving)
Through thick and thin	Through good and bad times
Thumbnail sketch	A brief or small picture or description
Time flies	Time passes very quickly
Tip of the iceberg	Only the part of something that can be easily observed, but not the rest of it, which is hidden
To the letter	Exactly as instructed; exactly as written
Tout suite!	Right away, with all haste
Tunnel vision	A visual impairment wherein one can only see what is directly ahead of oneself
Two shakes of lamb's tale	Quickly; rapidly
Two-time loser	A confirmed loser; a person who has already failed at a previous attempt at some task

Two-way street	A reciprocal situation
Under a cloud	Suspected of something
Under a spell	Enchanted; under magic's control
Unsung hero	A hero has gotten no praise or recognition
Until the cows come home	Until the last; until very late
Up for grabs	Available for anyone
User friendly	Easy to use
Vent spleen	To get rid of one's feelings of anger cause by someone or something by attacking someone or something else
Vested interest in	A personal or biased interest, often financial, in something
Vim and vigor	Energy; enthusiasm
Visit from the stork	A birth
Wait for the other shoe to drop	Wait for the inevitable next step or final conclusion
Wait-and-see attitude	A skeptical attitude; an uncertain attitude in which someone will just wait to see what happened before reacting
Wake up and smell the coffee	To become aware and sense what is going on around oneself
Waltz around	To move around or through a place happily or proudly

Warts and all	In spite of the flaws
Wax angry	To speak in anger
Wax poetic	To speak poetically
Whale the tar out of	To spank or beat someone
Wheel and deal	To take part in clever business deals
Whipping boy	Someone who is punished for someone else's misdeeds
Whistle in the dark	To guess aimlessly; to speculate as to a fact
White knuckle	To survive something threatening through strained endurance, that is to say, holding on tight
White-collar	Of the class of salaried office workers or lower-level managers
Whole shebang	Everything; the whole thing
With bells on (toes)	Eagerly, willingly, on time
With hat in hand	With humility
Work fingers to the bone	To work very hard
Worth salt	Worth what it costs to keep or support someone
Wrapped up	Involved with someone or something
Writer's block	The temporary inability for a writer to think of what to write

Ye gods (and little fishes)	What a surprising thing!
Yoke around neck	Something that oppresses people; a burden
You asked for it	You're getting what you requested
Young at heart	Having a youthful spirit no matter what one's age
Zero in	To aim directly at someone or something
Zero tolerance	Absolutely no toleration of even the small infraction of a rule
Zip your lip	Be quiet! Close your mouth and be quiet!

English Idioms and Phrases

A1	Excellent; first-rate
From A to Z	Over the entire range; in every particular
As easy (or simple) as ABC	Extremely easy or straightforward
Give someone the screaming abdabs	Induce an attack of extreme anxiety or irritation in someone
In Abraham's bosom	In heaven
Of your own accord	Voluntarily or without outside intervention
Settle (for square) accounts with someone	Have revenge on someone
Have an ace up your sleeve	Have a secret advantage
Hold all the aces	Have all the advantages
Within an ace of	Very close to
An Achilles heel	A person's only vulnerable spot; a serious or fatal weakness

Run amok	Behave uncontrollably and disruptively
In apple-pie order	In perfect order
Seal (or stamp)	Of approval; accepted or regarded favourably
Tied to someone's apron strings	A man too much under the influence of his mother
Argue the toss	Dispute a decision or choice already made
Out of the ark	Extremely old-fashioned
Cost an arm and a leg	Be extremely expensive
Keep someone or something at arm's length	Avoid intimacy or close contact with someone
The long arm of coincidence	The far reaching power of coincidence
The long (or strong) arm of the law	The power of the police
Up in arms	Protesting angrily about something
With open arms	With great affection or enthusiasm
An armchair critic	A person who knows about a subject only by reading or hearing about it; criticizes without active experience or first-hand knowledge

An atmosphere that you could cut with a knife	A general feeling of great tension
For auld lang syne	For old times' sake
Under the auspices of	With the help, support or protection of
Away with something	To be rid of something
Get away with you	To get unnoticed with what you have done
The awkward age	Adolescence
Have an axe to grind	Have a private motive for doing or being involved in something
The ayes have it	The affirmative votes are in the majority
Plan B	An alternative strategy
Babe in arms	An innocent, inexperienced, or gullible person; someone very young or new
Babes in the wood	Inexperienced people in a situation calling for experience
Throw the baby out with bathwater	Discard something valuable along with other things that are inessential or undesirable
At the back of your mind	Not consciously or specifically thought of or remembered but still part of your general awareness

A back number	An issue of a periodical before the current one
Back to the drawing board	An idea or scheme that has been unsuccessful and a new one must be devised
Back to square one	Back to the starting point, with no progress made
Back the wrong horse	Make a wrong or inappropriate choice
Behind someone's back	Without a person's knowledge and in an unfair or dishonorable way
By the back door	Using indirect or dishonest means to achieve an objective
Get someone's back up	Make someone annoyed or angry
Know something like the back of your hand	Be entirely familiar with something
See the back of	Be rid of an unwanted person or thing
Take a back seat	Take or be given a less important position or role
Turn your back on	Ignore
Put backbone into someone	Encourage someone to behave resolutely
To the backbone	In every respect; through and through

A back-seat driver	A passenger in a vehicle who constantly gives the driver unwanted advice on how to drive; someone who lectures and criticizes the person actually in control of something
Bend over backwards to do something	Make every effort, especially to be fair or helpful
Know something backwards	Be entirely familiar with something
Bring home the bacon	Achieve success
Bad hair day	A day on which everything seems to go wrong
A bad quarter of an hour	A short but very unpleasant period of time; an unnerving experience
Bag and baggage	With all your belongings
A bag of bones	An emaciated person or animal
A bag (or bundle) of nerves	A person who is extremely timid or tense
A baker's dozen	Thirteen
In the balance	Uncertain; at a critical stage
On balance	When all factors have been taken into consideration
Weigh something in the balance	Carefully ponder or assess the merits and demerits of something

When the band begins to play	When matters become serious
Jump on the bandwagon	Join others in doing something or supporting a cause that is fashionable or likely to be successful
Bang on	Exactly right
Get a bang out of	Derive excitement or pleasure from
Go with a bang	Happen with obvious success
Someone's bark is worse than their bite	Someone is not as ferocious as they appear or sound
A barrel of laughs	A source of fun or amusement
Get someone over a barrel	Get someone in a helpless position; have someone at your mercy
Man (or go to) the barricades	Strongly protest against a government or other institution or its policy
Get to first base	Achieve the first step towards your objective
Touch base	Briefly make or renew contact with someone or something
Have a bash	Make an attempt; try
Back to basics	To concentrate on the most essential aspects of something
Have had a basinful	Have had more than enough; wish to have no more
Basket case	A person or thing regarded as useless or unable to cope

Bat a thousand	Be enjoying great success
Like a bat out of hell	Very fast and wildly
Not bat an eyelid (or eye)	Show no emotional or other reaction
Off your own bat	Spontaneously
With bated breath	Very anxiously or excitedly
Pass (or hand) on the baton	Hand over a particular duty or responsibility
Battle of the giants	A contest between two pre-eminent parties
Battle royal	A fiercely contested fight or dispute
Half the battle	An important step towards achieving something
Hold (or keep) someone or something at bay	Prevent someone or something from approaching or having an effect
The be-all and end-all	A feature of an activity or a way of life
A beam in your eye	A fault that is greater in yourself than in the person you are finding fault with
On your beam ends	Near the end of your resources; desperate
Full of beans	Lively; in high spirits

Beat the system	Succeed in finding a means of getting round rules, regulations, or other means of control
Beat someone to it	Succeed in doing something or getting somewhere before someone else, to their annoyance
If you can't beat them, join them	If you are unable to outdo rivals in some endeavour, you might as well cooperate with them and gain whatever advantage possible by doing so
To beat the band	In such a way as to surpass all competition
Beaten (or pipped) at the post	Defeated at the last moment
Off the beaten track (or path)	Unusual
The beautiful people	Fashionable, glamorous, and privileged people
The body beautiful	An ideal of physical beauty
Work like a beaver	Work steadily and industriously
At someone's beck and call	Always having to be ready to obey someone's orders immediately
Bed and breakfast	Overnight accommodation and breakfast next morning as offered by hotels etc.

A bed of nails	A problematic or uncomfortable situation
A bed of roses	A situation or activity that is comfortable or easy
Fall out of bed	Suffer financial or commercial collapse
Get out of bed on the wrong side	Be bad tempered all day long
You have made your bed and must lie in it	You must accept the consequence of your own actions
Between you and me and the bedpost (or the gatepost or the wall)	In strict confidence
Have a bee in your bonnet	Have an obsessive preoccupation with something
Where's the beef?	Used to complain that something is too insubstantial
Make a beeline for	Go rapidly and directly towards
Beer and skittles	Amusement
Beggar belief (or description)	Be too extraordinary to be believed (or described)
Beggar on horseback	A formerly poor person made arrogant or corrupt through achieving wealth and luxury

Your best bib and tucker	Your best clothes
Bide your time	Wait quietly for a good opportunity
A big cheese	An important and influential person
Make it big	Become very successful or famous
Think big	Be ambitious
Bill and coo	Exchange caresses or affectionate words; behave or talk in a very loving or sentimental way
Fit (or fill) the bill	Be suitable for a particular purpose
Foot the bill	Be responsible for paying for something
Sell someone a bill of goods	Deceive or swindle someone, usually by persuading them to accept something untrue or undesirable
The bird has flown	The person you are looking for has escaped or gone away
A bird in hand	Something that you have secured or are sure of
A bird of passenger	Someone who is always moving on
A bird's-eye view	A general view from above
Birds of a feather	People with similar tastes, interests
Flip someone the bird	Stick your middle finger up at someone as a sign of contempt or anger

A little bird told me	Used as a teasing way of saying that you do not intend to divulge how you came to know something
Strictly for the birds	Not worth consideration; unimportant
In your birthday suit	Naked
Have had the biscuit	Be no longer good for anything; be done for
Bits and pieces (or bobs)	An assortment of small or unspecified items
Do your bit	Make a useful contribution to an effort or cause
Get the bit between your teeth	Begin to tackle a problem or task in a determined or independent way
Not a bit of it	Not at all; on the contrary
Bite the bullet	Face up to doing something difficult or unpleasant; stoically avoid showing fear or distress
Bite the dust	Be killed, fail
Bite the hand that feeds you	Deliberately hurt or offend a benefactor; act ungratefully
Bite of more than you can chew	Take on a commitment you cannot fulfil
Bite your tongue	Make a desperate effort to avoid saying something

Take a bite out of	Reduce by a significant amount
I could have bitten my tongue off	Used to convey that you profoundly and immediately regret having said something
Be in someone's black books	Be in disfavour with someone
Black and blue	Covered in bruises, (as if) from a severe beating
The black sheep	A person considered to have brought discredit upon a family or other group; a bad character
A black spot	A place that is notorious for something, especially a high crime or accident rate
In black and white	1. In writing or in print, and regarded as more reliable than by word of mouth 2. In terms of clearly defined opposing principles or issues
Blackboard jungle	A school, or schools in general, with violent and uncontrollable pupils
A blank cheque	Unlimited scope, especially to spend money
Draw a blank	Elicit no response; be unsuccessful
Born on the wrong side of the blanket	Illegitimate

Have kissed the blarney stone	Be eloquent and persuasive
A blast from the past	Something powerfully nostalgic, especially an old pop song
Bleeding heart	A person considered to be dangerously soft-hearted, typically someone too liberal or left-wing in their political beliefs
My heart bleeds for you	I sympathize very deeply with you
A blessing in disguise	An apparent misfortune that eventually has good results
A blind alley	A course of action that does not deliver any positive results
As blind as a bat	Having very bad eyesight
A blind date	A social meeting, usually with the object of starting a romance, between two people who have not met each other before
A blind spot	1. An area into which you cannot see 2. An aspect of something that someone knows or cares little about
Blind someone with science	Use special or technical knowledge and vocabulary to confuse someone
Turn a blind eye	Pretend not to notice
In the blink of an eye	Very quickly

Make your blood run cold	Horrify you
Someone's blood is up	Someone is in a fighting mood
Taste blood	Achieve an early success that stimulates further efforts
There is bad blood between	There is longstanding hostility between the parties mentioned
The bloom is off the rose	Something is on longer new, fresh or exciting
Blot your copybook	Tarnish your good reputation
A blot on the landscape	Something ugly that spoils the appearance of a place; an eyesore
Big girl's blouse	A weak, cowardly, or oversensitive man
Blow your cool	Lose your composure; become angry or agitated
Blow the doors off	Be considerably better or more successful than
Blow a fuse	Lose your temper
Blow hot and cold	Alternate inconsistently between two moods, attitudes, or courses of action; be sometime enthusiastic sometimes unenthusiastic about something
Blow someone's mind	Affect someone very strongly
Blow something sky-high	Destroy something completely in an explosion

Blow your top	Lose your temper
Blow up in your face	Go drastically wrong with damaging effects to yourself (of an action, plan, or situation)
Blow with the wind	Act according to prevailing circumstances rather than a consistent plan
I'll be blowed	Used to express surprise, annoyance, etc.
A blow-by-blow account	A detailed narrative of events as they happened
Be blown off course	Have your plans disrupted by some circumstance
Be blown out of the water	Be shown to lack credibility or viability (of a person idea, or project)
Do something until you are blue in the face	Persist in trying your hardest at an activity but without success
Once in a blue moon	Very rarely; practically never
Out of the blue	Without warning; very unexpectedly
Talk a blue streak	Speak continuously and at great length
A blue-eyed boy	The favourite of someone in authority
Blue sky research	Research that is not directed towards any immediate or definite commercial goal
Spare (or save) someone's blushes	Refrain from causing someone embarrassment

A bolt from the blue	A sudden and unexpected event or piece of news
Make a bolt for	Try to escape by moving suddenly towards something
A bone of contention	A subject or issue over which there is continuing disagreement
Cut (or pare) something to the bone	Reduce something to the bare minimum
Have a bone to pick with someone	Have reason to disagree or be annoyed with someone
Make no bones about something	Having no hesitation in stating or dealing with something, however unpleasant, awkward, or distasteful it is
To the bone	1. So deep as to expose the victim's bone (of a wound) 2. Affecting a person in a very penetrating way
Work your fingers to the bone	Work very hard
Bring someone to book	Bring someone to justice, punish someone
By the book	Strictly according to the rules
Close the book	Make no further entries at the end of an accounting period; cease trading
In someone's bad (or good) books	In disfavour (or favour) with some-one

Throw the book at	Charge or punish someone as severely as possible or permitted
The boot is on the other foot	The situation has reversed
Get the boot	Be dismissed from your job or position
Seven-league boots	The ability to travel very fast on foot
Your heart sinks into your boots	Used to express a feeling of sudden sadness or dismay
Pull (or drag) yourself up by your own bootstraps	Improve your position by your own efforts
Shake your booty	Dance energetically
Born and bred	By birth and upbringing
I wasn't born yesterday	Used to indicate that you are not foolish or gullible
Borrow trouble	Take needless action that may have bad effects
Living on borrowed time	Continuing to survive against expectations (used with the implication that this will not be much longer)
Borrowed plumes	A pretentious display not rightly your own
Show someone who's boss	Make it clear that it is yourself who is in charge

Hit (or be on) the bottle	Start to drink alcohol heavily
Bottoms up!	Used to express friendly feelings towards your companions before drinking
Get to the bottom of	Find an explanation for (a mystery)
Bounce an idea off someone	Share an idea with another person in order to get feedback on it and refine it
Bounce off the walls	Be full of nervous excitement or agitation
A bounden duty	A responsibility regarded by yourself or others as obligatory
Make your bow	Make your first formal appearance in a particular role
Take a bow	1. Acknowledge applause after a performance (of an actor or entertainer) 2. Used to tell someone that they should feel themselves worthy of applause
Back in your box	No longer conspicuous or calling attention to yourself; returned to a low profile
Box clever	Act so as to outwit someone
Be a box of birds	Be fine or happy
In the wrong box	Placed unsuitably or awkwardly; in difficulty or at a disadvantage

The big boys	Men or organizations considered to be most powerful
Boys will be boys	Childish, irresponsible Or mischievous behaviour is typical of boys or young men
Have something on the brain	Be obsessed with something
Brass monkey	Used in various phrases to refer to extremely cold weather
The brass ring	Success, especially as a reward for ambition or hard word
Get (or come) down to brass tacks	Start to consider the essential facts or practical details; reach the real matter in hand
Brave new world	A new and hopeful period in history resulting from major changes in society
Step into the breach	Take the place of someone who is suddenly unable to do a job or task
The best (or greatest) thing since sliced bread	A notable new idea, person or thing (used to express real or ironic appreciation)
Break bread with	Share a meal with someone
Cast your bread upon the waters	Do good without expecting gratitude or immediate reward

Eat the bread of idleness	Eat food that you have not worked for
Have your bread buttered on both sides	Be in a state of easy prosperity
Know on which side your bread is buttered	Know where your advantage lies
Man cannot live by bread alone	People have spiritual as well as physical needs
Someone's bread and butter	Someone's livelihood; routine work to provide an income
Take the bread out of people's mouths	Deprive people of their livings, especially by competition or unfair working practices
Want your bread buttered on both sides	Want more than is practicable or than is reasonable to expect
A bread-and-butter letter	A guest's written thanks for hospitality
Break the back of	1. Accomplish the main or hardest part of a task 2. Overwhelm or defeat
Break a butterfly on a wheel	Use unnecessary force in destroying something fragile or insignificant
Break even	Reach a point in a business venture where the profits are equal to the costs

Break some-one's heart	Overwhelm someone with sadness
Break a leg!	Good luck!
Give someone a break	Stop putting pressure on someone about something
Make a break for	Make a sudden dash in the direction of, usually in a bid to escape
You're breaking my heart	Used ironically to suggest that the person referred to does not deserve the sympathy they are seeking
Beat your breast	Make a great show of sorrow or regret
The breath of life	A thing that someone needs or depends on
In the same (or the next) breath	As the next in a series of statements, contradicting a previous one
Save your breath	Not bother to say something because it is pointless
Take someone's breath away	Inspire someone with awed respect or delight; astonish someone
Under your breath	In a very quiet voice; almost in-audibly
Waste your breath	Talk or give advice without effect
Breathe down someone's neck	Constantly check up on someone; follow closely behind someone
Breathe your last	Die

A breed apart	A kind of person or thing that is very different form the norm
A brick short of a load	Stupid (of a person)
Make bricks without straw	Try to accomplish something without proper or adequate material, equipment, or information
Always the bridesmaid	Used to refer pityingly to someone who seems always to be allocated to a subsidiary function, and is never invited to take the lead
Cross that bridge when you come to it	Deal with a problem when and if it arises
Hold no brief for	Not support or argue in favour of
Bright and early	Very early in the morning
As bright as a button	Intelligently alert and lively
The bright lights	The glamour and excitement of a big city
Bright young thing	A wealthy, pleasure loving, and fashionable young person
Bright-eyed and bushy-tailed	Alert and lively; eager
Bring the house down	Make an audience respond with great enthusiasm, especially as shown by their laughter or applause

Bring something into play	Cause something to begin to have an effect
In broad daylight	Used generally to express surprise or outrage at someone's daring to carry out a particular act, especially a crime, during the day, when anyone could see it
A new broom	A newly appointed person who is likely to make far-reaching changes
Big brother	The state perceived as a sinister force supervising citizens' lives
As brown as a berry	Very suntanned (of a person)
Brownie point	An imaginary award given to someone who does good deeds or tries to please
Bear the brunt of	Be the person to suffer the most
On the bubble	Occupying the last qualifying position in a team or for a tournament, and liable to be replaced by another
The buck stops here (or with someone)	The responsibility for something cannot or should not be passed to someone else
Make a fast buck	Earn money easily and quickly
Pass the buck	Shift the responsibility for something to someone else
In the buff	Naked

Like a bull at a gate	Hastily and without thought
Like a bull in a china shop	Behaving recklessly and clumsily in a place or situation where you are likely to cause damage or injury
Bumper-to-bumper	Very close together, as cars in a traffic jam
Have a bun in the oven	Be pregnant
Bundle of joy	A baby, especially one who is newly born or whose birth is keenly anticipated
A bundle of fun (or laughs)	Something extremely amusing or pleasant
Drop your bundle	Panic or lose one's self-control
Go bung	Fail or go bankrupt
Give it a burl	Attempt to do something
Burn your boats (or bridges)	Commit yourself irrevocably
Burn the candle at both ends	Lavish resources in more than one direction at the same time
Burn the midnight oil	Read or work late into the night
Go for the burn	Push your body to the extremes when practicing a form of physical exercise
On the back (or front) burner	Having low (or high) priority

Burnt to a cinder (or crisp)	Completely burnt through, leaving only the charred remnant
Burst someone's bubble	Shatter someone's illusions about something or destroy their sense of well-being
Bury the hatchet	End a quarrel or conflict and become friendly
Bury your head in the sand	Ignore unpleasant realities; refuse to face facts
Like the back of a bus	Very ugly (of a face)
Like nobody's business	In no ordinary way; to an extremely intense degree
A busman's holiday	A holiday or form of recreation that involves doing the same thing that you do at work
A busted flush	Someone or something that has not fulfilled expectations; a failure
Bust a gut	Make a strenuous effort
As busy as a bee	Very busy or industrious
Busy bee	An industrious person
Look as if butter wouldn't melt in your mouth	Appear deceptively gentle or innocent
Have (or be a) butterfingers	Be unable to catch deftly or hold securely

The butterfly effect	The phenomenon whereby a minute localized change in a complex system can have large effects elsewhere
Have butterflies in your stomach	Have a queasy feeling because you are nervous
On the button	Punctually; exactly right
Push (or press) someone's buttons	Be successful in arousing or provoking a reaction in someone
By and large	On the whole; everything considered
By the by (or bye)	Incidentally; parenthetically
Let bygones be bygones	Forgive and forget past offences or causes of conflict
Cut the cackle	Stop talking aimlessly and come to the point
Ceasar's wife	A person who is required to be above suspicion
In cahoots	Working or conspiring together, often dishonestly; in collusion
Cakes and ale	Merrymaking
You can't have your cake and eat it	You can't enjoy both of two desirable but mutually exclusive alternatives
Sell (or go) like hot cakes	Be sold quickly and in large quantities
Call the shots (or tune)	Take the initiative in deciding how something should be done; be in control

Cannot hold a candle to	Be nowhere near as good as
Cap in hand	Humbly asking for a favour
Carbon copy	A person or thing identical or very similar to another
Get your cards	Be dismissed from your employment
Have a card up your sleeve	Have a plan or asset that is kept secret until it is needed
Hold all the cards	Be in the strongest or most advantageous position
Keep (or play) your cards close to your chest (or vest)	Be extremely secretive and cautious about something
On the cards	Possible or likely
Play your cards right	Make the best use of your assets and opportunities
Put (or lay) your cards on the table	Be completely open and honest in declaring your resources, intentions, or attitude
Not care two straws	Care little or not at all
Take care	Said to someone on leaving them
A magic carpet	A means of sudden and effortless travel
Sweep something under the carpet	Hide or ignore a problem or difficulty in the hope that it will be forgotten
Carrot and stick	The promise of reward combined with the threat of force or punishment

In the cart	In trouble or difficulty
Put the cart before the horse	Reverse the proper order or procedure of something
A case in point	An instance or example that illustrates what is being discussed
Cash in hand	Payment for goods and services by money in the form of notes and coins
Be cast in a – mould	Be of the type specified
Cast something in someone's teeth	Reject defiantly or refer reproachfully to a person's previous action or statement
Build castle in the air (or in Spain)	Have a visionary and unattainable scheme; daydream
All cats are grey in the dark	The qualities that distinguish people from one another are obscured in some circumstances, and if they can't be perceived they don't matter
The cat has got someone's tongue	Someone is remaining silent
A cat may look at a king	Even a person of low status or importance has rights
Enough to make a cat laugh	Extremely ridiculous or ironic
Fight like cat and dog	Be continually arguing with one another (of two people)
Let the cat out of the bag	Reveal a secret, especially carelessly or by mistake

Like a cat on a hot tin roof (or on hot bricks)	Very agitated, restless, or anxious
Not a cat in hell's chance	No chance at all
Play cat and mouse with	Manoeuvre in a way designed alternately to provoke and thwart an opponent
Put (or set) the cat among the pigeons	Say or do something that is likely to cause trouble or controversy
See which way the cat jumps	See what direction events are talking before committing yourself
That cat won't jump	That suggestion is implausible or impracticable
When the cat's away, the mice will play	People will naturally take advantage of the absence of someone in authority to do someone in authority to do as they like
In the catbird seat	In a superior or more advantageous position
Catch someone's eye	Be noticed by someone
Catch a tartar	Encounter or get hold of a person who can neither be controlled nor got rid of
A catch – 22 situation	A dilemma or difficulty from which there is no escape because of mutually conflicting or dependent conditions

Play catch-up	Try to equal a competitor in a sporting event
The cat's whiskers	An excellent person or thing
Make common cause with	Unite with in order to achieve a shared aim
Throw caution to the wind (or winds)	Act in a completely reckless manner
Keep cave	Act as lookout
Caviar to the general	A good thing that is not appreciated by the ignorant
Hit the ceiling	Fly into a sudden rage
Stand on ceremony	Insist on the observance of formalities; behave formally
Bad cess to	A curse on
Be caught with chaff	Be easily deceived
As different as chalk and cheese (or like chalk and cheese)	Fundamentally different or incompatible
Chalk and talk	Teaching by traditional methods focusing on the blackboard and presentation by the teacher as opposed to more informal or interactive methods

Champ (or chafe) at the bit	Be restlessly impatient, especially to start doing something
Chance your arm (or luck)	Undertake something although it may be dangerous or unsuccessful; take a risk
On the off chance	Just in case
A change is as good as a rest	A change of work or occupation can be as restorative or refreshing as a period of relaxation
A change of heart	A move to a different opinion or attitude
Change your tune	Express a very different opinion or behave in a very different way
Ring the changes	Vary the ways of expressing, arranging, or doing, something
Return to the charge	Make a further attempt at something, especially in arguing a point
Charity begins at home	A person's first responsibility is for the needs of their own family and friends
Work like a charm	Be completely successful or effective
The chattering classes	Articulate and educated people considered as a social group given to the expression of liberal opinions about society and culture
Cheap and cheerful	Simple and inexpensive

An old chestnut	A joke, story, or subject that has become tedious and boring as a result of its age and constant repetition
Pull someone's chestnuts out of the fire	Succeed in a hazardous undertaking for someone else's benefit
A chicken-and-egg problem	An unresolved question as to which of two things caused the other
Chickens come home to roost	Your past mistake or wrongdoings will eventually be the cause of present troubles
Chicken feed	A paltry sum of money
No (spring) chicken	Not a young person
Running (or rushing) about like a headless chicken	Acting in a panic –stricken manner and not thinking clearly about what should be done
Big white chief	A person in authority
Chief cook and bottle-washer	A person who performs a variety of important but routine tasks
Child's play	A task which is very easily accomplished
Keep your chin up	Remain cheerful in difficult circumstances
Take it on the chin	Endure or accept misfortune courageously
Not a chinaman's chance	Not even a very slight chance

A chink in someone's armour	A weak point in someone's character, argument, or ideas which makes them vulnerable to attack or criticism
A chip off the old block	Someone who resembles his parent, especially in character
A chip on your shoulder	A strong and usually long-standing inclination to feel resentful
Have had your chips	Be dead, dying, or out of contention
When the chips are down	When you find yourself in a very serious and difficult situation
Hobson's choice	No choice at all
Bust someone's chops	Nag or criticize someone
Bust your chops	Expert yourself
Chop and change	Change your opinions or behaviour repeatedly
Chop logic	Argue in a tiresomely pedantic way; quibble
Not much chop	No good; not up to much
Strike (or touch) a chord	Say or do something which affects or stirs the emotions of others
Chuck it down	Rain heavily
Off your chump	Crazy
Circle the wagons	Unite in defence of a common interest (of a group)

Come (or turn) full circle	Return to a past position or situation, often in a way considered to be inevitable
Go round in circles	Do something for a long time without achieving anything but purposeless repetition
Run round in circle	Be fussily busy with little result
The wheel has turned (or come) full circle	The situation has returned to what it was in the past, as if completing a cycle
Citizen of the world	A person who is at home in any country
Keep a civil tongue in your head	Speak politely and calmly, without rudeness
Claim to fame	A reason for being regarded as unusual or noteworthy
Clap someone in jail (or irons)	Put someone in prison (or in chains)
Like the clappers	Very fast or very hard
Tap someone's claret	Make someone's nose bleed by a blow with the fist
A class act	A person or thing displaying impressive and stylish excellence
Get your claws into	Enter into a possessive relationship with someone (used especially of a woman who dominates or manipulates a man)

Clean as a whistle	Extremely clean or clear
Clean someone's clock	Give someone a beating
Clean house	Eliminate corruption or inefficiency
Clean up your act	Behave in a more acceptable manner
Come clean	Be completely honest and frank
Make a clean breast of something (or of it)	Confess your mistakes or wrong-doings
Make a clean sweep	Remove all unwanted people or things ready to start afresh
Mr Clean	An honourable or incorruptible politician
Take someone to the cleaners	Take all of someone's money or possessions in a dishonest or unfair way
Clear blue water	An obvious and decisive gap between you and your rivals
Clear your desk	Leave your job, especially having been dismissed
Clear as mud	Not at all easy to understand
Clear the decks	Prepare for a particular event or goal by dealing beforehand with anything that might hinder progress
Be (or be caught) in a cleft stick	Be in a difficult situation, when any action you take will have adverse consequences
Click into place	Become suddenly clear and understandable

Be climbing the walls	Feel frustrated
At a clip	At a time; all at once
Clip someone's wings	Prevent someone from acting freely
Round (or around) the clock	All day and all night; ceaselessly
Turn back the clock	Return to the past or to a previous way of doing things
Watch the clock	Wait eagerly for the end of working hours
Like clockwork	Very smoothly and easily with no disruptions or problems
Clogs to clogs in three generations	The return of a family to poverty after one generation of prosperity
Close shave (or call)	A narrow escape from danger or disaster
Too close for comfort	Dangerously or uncomfortably near
Behind closed doors	Done in a secretive or furtive way; hidden from public view
A closed book	A thing of which you have no knowledge or understanding
Out of the closet	Out into the open
Cloth ears	An inability to hear or understand clearly
On cloud nine	Extremely happy

A cock-and-bull story	A ridiculous and implausible story
Cock of the walk	Someone who dominates others within a group
Warm the cockles of someone's heart	Give someone a comforting feeling of pleasure or contentment
Bring something up to code	Renovate an old building or update its features in line with the latest building regulations
Coign of vantage	A favourable position for observation or action
Shuffle off this mortal coil	Die
The other side of the coin	The opposite or contrasting aspect of a matter
Pay someone back in their own coin	Retaliate by similar behaviour
To coin a phrase	Said ironically when introducing a banal remark or cliché
Cold comfort	Poor or inadequate consolation
Cold feet	Loss of nerve or confidence
In the cold light of day	When you have had time to consider a situation objectively
The cold shoulder	A show of intentional unfriendliness; rejection

Go cold turkey	Suddenly and completely stop taking drugs
Have someone cold	Have someone at your mercy
In cold blood	Without feeling or mercy; ruthlessly
Left out in the cold	Ignored; neglected
Out cold	Completely unconscious
Pour (or throw) cold water on	Be discouraging or negative about a plan or suggestion
Feel someone's collar	Arrest or legally apprehend someone
On a collision course	Adopting an approach that is certain to lead to conflict
Lend (or give) colour to	Make something seem true or probable
See the colour of someone's money	Receive some evidence of forthcoming payment from a person
Nail (or pin) your colours to mast	Declare openly and firmly what you believe or favour
Sail under false colours	Disguise your true nature or intentions
Come in from the cold	Gain acceptance
Common or garden	Of the usual or ordinary type

Be (or err) in good company	Be in the same situation as someone important or respected
Conspicuous by your absence	Obviously not present in a place where you should be
A conspiracy of silence	An agreement to say nothing about an issue that should be generally known
To your heart's content	To the full extent of your desires
Within cooee of	Within reach of; near to
Cook the books	Alter records, especially accounts, with fraudulent intent or in order to mislead
Cook someone's goose	Spoil someone's plans; cause someone's downfall
Too many cooks spoil the broth	If too many people are involved in a task or activity, it will not be done well
The way (or how) the cookie crumbles	How things turn out (often used of an undesirable but unalterable situation)
With your hand in the cookie jar	Engaged in surreptitious theft from your employer
Cut the cord	Cease to rely on someone or something influential or supportive and begin to act independently
Corn in Egypt	A plentiful supply
Fight your corner	Defend your position or interests

The corridors of power	The senior levels of government or administration, where covert influence is regarded as being exerted and significant decisions are made
Wrap someone in cotton wool	Be over-protective towards someone
Couch potato	Someone who watches a lot of television, eats junk food, and takes little or no physical exercise
A counsel of despair	An action to be taken when all else fails
A counsel of perfection	Advice that is ideal but not feasible
Count your blessings	Be grateful for what you have
Count your chickens	Treat something that has not yet happened as a certainty
Count something on the fingers of one hand	Used to emphasize the small number of a particular thing
Count to ten	Count to ten under your breath in order to prevent yourself from reacting angrily to something
Out for the count	Unconscious or soundly asleep
Take the count	Be knocked out (of a boxer)
Out of countenance	Disconcerted or unpleasantly surprised

Over the counter	By ordinary retail
A country mile	A very long way; a very large margin
Line of country	A subject about which a person is skilled or knowledgeable
Take your courage in both hands	Nerve yourself to do something that frightens you
Blow someone's cover	Discover or expose someone's real identity
Cover the waterfront	Cover every aspect of something
Cover your back	Foresee and avoid the possibility of attack or criticism
Cover your tracks	Conceal evidence of what you have done
Till the cows come home	For an indefinitely long time
Crack a book	Open a book and read it; study
Crack a crib	Break into a house
Crack of doom	A peal of thunder announcing the day of judgement
A fair crack of a whip	Fair treatment; a chance to participate or compete on equal terms
Get cracking	Act quickly and energetically
From the cradle to the grave	All through a person's life, from beginning to end

Cramp someone's style	Prevent a person from acting freely or naturally
Cream your jeans	Experience strong emotions of delight and excitement
Creature of habit	A person who follows an unvarying routine
Credit where credit is due	Praise should be given when it is deserved, even when you are reluctant to give it
Be up the creek without a paddle	Be in severe difficulty, usually with no means of extricating yourself from it
Give someone the creeps	Induce a feeling of fear or revulsion in someone
On the crest of a wave	At a very successful point
Not cricket	Contrary to traditional standards of fairness or rectitude
Crocodile tears	A display of insincere grief
At cross purposes	Misunderstanding or having different aims from one another
Cross as two sticks	Very annoyed or grumpy
Cross your fingers (or keep your fingers crossed)	Hope that your plans will be successful; trust in good luck
Cross the floor	Join the opposing side in parliament

Cross my heart	Used to emphasize the truthfulness and sincerity or what you are saying or promising
Cross swords	Have an argument or dispute
Have your cross to bear	Suffer the troubles that life brings
Get your wires (or lines) crossed	Have a misunderstanding
Be caught in the crossfire	Suffer damage or harm inadvertently as the result of the conflict between two other people or groups
At a (or the) crossroads	At a critical point, when decisions with far-reaching consequences must be made
As the crow flies	Used to refer to a shorter distance in a straight line across country
Crowning glory	The best and most notable aspect of something
Cruising for a bruising	Heading or looking for trouble
Cry stinking fish	Disparage your own efforts or products
In full cry	Expressing an opinion loudly and forcefully
For crying out loud	Used to express your irritation or impatience
Cuckoo in the nest	An unwelcome intruder in a place or situation

Cudgel your brain (or brains)	Think hard about a problem
Take your cue from	Follow the example or advice of
Off the cuff	Without preparation
Culture vulture	A person who is very interested in the arts, especially to an obsessive degree
In your cups	While drunk
Not your cup of tea	Not what you like or are interested in
A curate's egg	Something that is partly good and partly bad
Curiosity killed the cat	Being inquisitive about other people's affairs may get you into trouble
Make someone's hair curl	Shock or horrify someone
Pass current	Be generally accepted as true or genuine
Curry favour	Do a favour to get an immediate return
Bring down the curtain on	Bring to an end
Throw a curve	Cause confusion by acting unexpectedly
A cut above	Superior to
Be cut out for (or to be)	Have exactly the right qualities for a particular role, task, or job

Cut and dried	Completely settled or decided (of a situation, issue, or ideas)
Cut corners	Undertake something in what appears to be the easiest way by ignoring rules
Cut the crap	Get to the point; state the real situation
Cut a dash	Be stylish or impressive in your dress or behaviour
Cut someone dead	Completely ignore someone
Cut a deal	Come to an arrangement especially in business; make a deal
Cut someone down to size	Deflate someone's exaggerated sense of self-worth
Cut from the same cloth	Of the same nature
Cut it	Meet the required standard
Cut the Gordian knot	Solve or remove a problem in a direct or forceful way, rejecting gentler or more indirect methods
Cut the mustard	Come up to expectations; meet the required standard
Cut no ice	Have no influence or effect
The cut of someone's jib	The appearance or look of a person
Cut your teeth	Acquire initial practice or experience of a particular sphere of activity or with a particular organization

A dark horse	A person, especially a competitor, about whom little is known
Keep someone in the dark	Ensure that someone remains in a state of ignorance about something
A shot (or stab) in the dark	An act whose outcome cannot be foreseen; a mere guess
Never darken someone's door (or doorstep)	Keep away from someone's home permanently
Go to Davy Jones's locker	Be drowned at sea
All in a day's work	Accepted as part of someone's normal routine
Any day	At any time
Call it a day	Decide or agree to stop doing something
Carry (or win) the day	Be victorious or successful
Day in, day out	Continuously or repeatedly over a long period of time
Day of reckoning	The time when past mistakes or misdeeds must be punished or paid for
From day one	From the very beginning
One of those days	A day when several things go wrong
Beat the (living) daylights out of	Give someone a very severe beating

Daylight robbery	Blatant and unfair overcharging
Dead and buried	Used to emphasize that something is finally and irrevocably in the past
Dead as a doornail (or as mutton)	Completely dead
A dead cat bounce	A misleading sign of vitality in something that is really moribund
Dead from the neck (or chin) up	Stupid
Dead in the water	Unable to function effectively
A dead letter	A law or practice no longer observed
Dead meat	In serious trouble
Dead to the world	Fast asleep; unconscious
Dead wood	People or things that are no longer useful or productive
Over my dead body	Used to emphasize that you completely oppose something
Deaf as an adder (or a post)	Completely or extremely deaf
A big deal	A thing considered important
A square deal	A fair bargain or treatment
At death's door	So ill that you may die
Be frightened to death	Be made very alarmed and fearful

Hit the deck	Fall to or throw yourself on the ground
Delusions of grandeur	A false impression of your own importance
Get (or receive) your just deserts	Receive what you deserve, especially appropriate punishment
Have designs on	Aim to obtain something desired, especially in an underhand way
Like the deuce	Very fast
Leave someone to their own devices	Leave someone to do as they wish without supervision
Between the devil and the deep blue sea	Caught in a dilemma; trapped between two equally dangerous alternatives
The devil to pay	Serious trouble to be expected
Give the devil his due	If someone or something generally considered bad or undeserving has any redeeming features these should be acknowledged
Like the devil's advocate	Take a side in an argument that is the opposite of what you really want or think
Play the devil (or old Harry) with	Damage or affect greatly
Raise the devil	Make a noisy disturbance

Dialogue of the deaf	A discussion in which each party is unresponsive to what the others say
Diamond cuts diamond	A situation in which a sharp-witted or cunning person meets his match
Dice with death	Take serious risks
Not a dicky bird	Not a word; nothing at all
Have swallowed a dictionary	Use long and obscure words when speaking
Cut didoes	Perform mischievous tricks or deeds
Die hard	Disappear or change very slowly
Die in your bed	Suffer a peaceful death from natural causes
Die in the last ditch	Die desperately defending something; die fighting to the last extremity
Die like a dog	Die in degrading circumstances
Die on the vine	Be unsuccessful at an early stage
Die on your feet	Come to a sudden or premature end
Die with your boots on	Die while actively occupied
Never say die	Used to encourage someone not to give up hope in a difficult situation
Straight as a die	Entirely open and honest
To die for	Extremely good or desirable
Different stokes for different folks	Different things please or are effective with different people

Dig the dirt (or dig up dirt)	Discover and reveal damaging information about someone
Dig in your heels	Resist stubbornly; refuse to give in
Dig yourself into a hole (or dig a hole for yourself)	Get yourself into an awkward or restrictive situation
Dig your own grave	Do something foolish which causes you to fail or leads to your downfall
Dig a pit for	Try to trap
Beneath your dignity	Of too little importance or value for you to do it
A dime a dozen	Very common and of no particular value
By dint of	By means of
Dip your pen in gall	Write unpleasantly or spitefully
Dip you toe into something	Begin to do or test something cautiously
Do someone dirt	Harm someone maliciously
Treat someone like dirt	Treat someone contemptuously
The dirty end of the stick	The difficult or unpleasant part of a task or situation
Dirty work at the crossroads	Illicit or underhand dealing

A dog's dinner (or breakfast)	A poor piece of work; a mess
A dog's life	An unhappy existence full of problems or unfair treatment
Dog tired	Extremely tired; utterly worm out
Dogs of war	The havoc accompanying military conflict
Every dog has his (or its) day	Everyone will have good luck or success at some point in their lives
Give a dog a bad name	It is very difficult to lose a bad reputation, even if it is unjustified
Go to the dogs	Deteriorate shockingly, especially in behaviour or morals
Keep a dog and bark yourself	Pay someone to work for you and then do the work yourself
Let the dog see the rabbit	Let someone get on with work they are ready and waiting to do
Like a dog with two tails	Showing great pleasure; delighted
My dogs are barking	My feet are aching
You can't teach an old dog new tricks	You cannot make people change their ways
Donkey work	The boring or laborious part of a job; drudgery
For donkey's years	For a very long time
Doom and gloom	A general feeling of pessimism or despondency

As one door close, another opens	You shouldn't be discouraged by failure, as other opportunities will soon present themselves
Lay something at someone's door	Regard or name someone as responsible for something
Leave the door open for	Ensure that there is still an opportunity for something
On your (or the) doorstep	Very near; close at hand
In small doses	Experienced or engaged in a little at a time
Like a dose of salts	Very fast and efficiently
Dot the i's and cross the t's	Ensure that all details are correct
On the dot	Exactly on time
The year dot	A very long time ago
At (or on) the double	At running speed; very past
Double or nothing	A gamble to decide whether a loss or debt should be doubled or cancelled
A doubting Thomas	A person who refuse to believe something without having incontrovertible proof; a sceptic
Down and out	Beaten in the struggle of life; completely without resources or means of livelihood
Down on your luck	Experiencing a period of bad luck

Down the road	In the future; later on
On the downgrade	In decline
Drag your feet (or heels)	Be deliberately slow or reluctant to act (of a person or organization)
Drag someone or something through the dirt (or mud)	Make damaging allegations about someone or something
Down the drain	Totally wasted or spoilt
Feel the draught	Experience an adverse change in your financial circumstances
Draw the (or a) line at	Set a limit of what you are willing to do or accept, beyond which you will not go
Draw stumps	Cease doing something
Bottom drawer	The collection of linen, clothes, and household items assembled by a woman in preparation for her marriage
Beyond your wildest dreams	Bigger, better, or to a greater extent than it would be reasonable to expect or hope for
Dream in color (or Technicolor)	Be wildly unrealistic
Never in your wildest dreams	Used to emphasize that something is beyond the scope of your imagination

All dressed up and (or with) nowhere (or no place) to go	Prepared for action but having nothing to do or unable to be proceeded with
Dressed to kill	Wearing attractive and flamboyant clothes in order to make a striking impression
Drink like a fish	Drink excessive amounts of alcohol, especially habitually
In the driver's (or driving) seat	In charge of a situation
At the drop of a hat	On the slightest excuse
Drop your aitches	Fail to pronounce the 'h' sound, especially at the beginning of word
Drop the ball	Make a mistake; mishandle things
Drop a brick	Make an indiscreet or embarrassing remark
Drop dead	Die suddenly and unexpectedly
Drop a hint (or drop hints)	Let fall a hint or hints, as if casually or unconsciously
Drop someone a line	Send someone a note or letter in a causal manner
A drop in the ocean (or in a bucket)	A very small amount compared with what is needed or expected
Drown your sorrows	Forget your problems by getting drunk

Like a drowned rat	Extremely wet and bedraggled
A drug on the market	An unsaleable or valueless commodity
Dry as a bone	Extremely thirsty
Dry as dust	Extremely dry
Duck and dive	Use your ingenuity to deal with or evade a situation
Like a dying duck in a thunderstorm	Having a dejected or hopeless expression
Take to something like a duck to water	Take to something very readily
Play ducks and drakes with	Trifle with; treat frivolously
Duke it out	Fight it out
Never a dull moment	Used to express the idea of constant variety and excitement
Into the dumper	Into a bad or worse state or condition
Down in the dumps	Depressed or unhappy
Dust and ashes	Used to convey a feeling of great disappointment or disillusion about something
The dust settles	Things quieten down
Do the Dutch	Commit suicide

Dutch courage	Bravery induced by drinking alcohol
A Dutch wife	A bolster
A Dutch uncle	A kindly but authoritative figure
Go Dutch	Share the cost of something equally
In Dutch	In trouble
An eager beaver	A person who is very enthusiastic about work
Be all ears	Be listening eagerly and attentively
Bring something (down) about your ears	Bring something, especially misfortune, on yourself
Have someone's ear	Influence someone
Have something by the ears	Keep or obtain a secure hold on
Have something coming out of your ears	Have a substantial or excessive amount of something
Have (or keep) an ear to the ground	Be well informed about events and trends
Listen with half an ear	Not give your full attention
Someone's ears are burning	Someone is subconsciously aware of being talked about, especially in their absence
Someone's ears are flapping	Someone is listening intently in order to overhear something not intended for them
Early bird	A person who gets up, arrives, or acts before the usual or expected time

Early doors	Early on, especially in a game or contest
It's early days	It is too soon to be sure how a particular situation will develop
Earn your corn	Put in a lot of effort for your wages
Earn your keep	Be worth the time, money or effort spent on you
A nice little earner	A profitable activity or business
Cost (or charge or pay) the earth	Cost (or charge or pay) a large amount of money
Go to earth	Go into hiding
Like nothing on earth	Very strange
Not stand (or have) an earthly	Have no chance at all
Come easy to	Present little difficulty to
Easier said than done	More easily talked about than put into practice
Easy as falling off a log	Very easy
Easy as pie	Very easy
Easy come, easy go	Used to indicate that something acquired without effort or difficulty may be lost or spent casually and without regret
Easy does it	Approach a task carefully and slowly

Eat someone out of house and home	Eat a lot of someone else's food
Eat your words	Retract what you have said especially when forced to do so
I'll eat my hat	Used to indicate that you think a particular thing is extremely unlikely to happen
Have someone eating out of your hand	Have someone completely under your control
What's eating you (or him or her)?	What is worrying or annoying you
At a low ebb	In an especially poor state
Ebb and flow	A recurrent or rhythmical pattern of coming and going or decline and regrowth
Applaud (or cheer) someone to the echo	Applaud (or cheer) someone very enthusiastically
In eclipse	Losing or having lost significance, power, or prominence
Economical with the truth	Used euphemistically to describe a person or statement that lies or deliberately withholds information
On the edge of your seat (or chair)	Very excited and giving your full attention to something

Take the edge off something	Reduce the intensity or effect of something, especially something unpleasant or severe
Don't put all your eggs in one basket	Don't risk everything on the success of one venture
Go suck an egg	Go away
Lay an egg	Be completely unsuccessful; fail badly
Behind the eight ball	At a disadvantage; baffled
One over the eight	Slightly drunk
Give someone the elbow	Reject or dismiss someone
Out at elbows	Wearing shabby or ragged clothing
Up to your elbows in	Deeply involved in
The elephant in the corner	An embarrassing or awkward topic that everyone is aware of but no one wishes to discuss
See the elephant	See the world; get experience of life
At the eleventh hour	At the latest possible moment
The Elysian Fields	Heaven
Be running on empty	Have exhausted all your resources or sustenance

Empty nester	A person whose children have grown up and left home
Empty vessels make most noise (or sound)	Those with least wisdom or knowledge are always the most talkative
All ends up	Completely
At the end of the day	When everything is taken into consideration
At the end of your tether	Having no patience, resources, or energy left to cope with something
The end justifies the means	Wrong or unfair methods may be used if the overall goal is good
The ends of the earth	The most distant parts of the world
The end of the road (or line)	The point beyond which progress or survival cannot continue
End of story	Used to emphasize that there is nothing more to add on the subject just mentioned
The end of the world	A complete disaster
Keep (or hold) your end up	Perform well in a difficult or competitive situation
Make (both) ends meet	Earn or have enough money to live on without getting into debt
No end of something	A vast number or amount of something
Be your own worst enemy	Act contrary to your own interests; be self-destructive

Enough is as good as a feast	Moderation is more satisfying than excess
Enough said	There is no need to say more; all is understood
Push the envelope (or the edge of the envelope)	Approach or extend the limits of what is possible
First among equals	The person or thing having the highest status in a group
Other (or all) things being equal	Provided that other factors or circumstances remain the same
Err on the right side	Act so that the most likely mistake to be made is the least harmful one
Err on the side of	Act with a specified bias towards something
To err is human, to forgive divine	It is human nature to make mistakes yourself while finding it hard to forgive others
Of the essence	Critically important
The eternal city	A name for the city of Rome
Eternal triangle	A relationship between three people, typically a couple and the lover of one of them, involving sexual rivalry
An even break	A fair chance
Get (or be) even with	Inflict similar trouble or harm on someone as they have inflicted on you

Close (or shut) your eyes to	Defraud, thwart, or humiliate someone
Eyes out on stalks	Full of eager curiosity or amazement
Get (or keep) your eye in	Become (or remain) able to make good judgements about a task or occupation in which you are engaged
Give someone the (glad) eye	Look at someone in a way that clearly indicates your sexual interest in them
Go eyes out	Make every effort
Half an eye	A slight degree of perception or attention
Have an eye for	Be able to recognize, appreciate, and make good judgements about a particular thing
Have eyes in the back of your stomach	Have asked for or taken more food than you can actually eat
Have eyes in the back of your head	Observe everything that is happening even when this is apparently impossible
Have eyes like a hawk	Miss nothing of what is going on around you
Hit someone in the eye (or between the eyes)	Be very obvious or impressive
Keep an eye out (or open) for	Look out for something with particular attention

Give your eye teeth for	Go to any lengths in order to obtain something
A face as long as a fiddle	A dismal face
Face the music	Be confronted with the unpleasant consequences of your actions
Fact to face	In a position in which you must confront a difficulty
Get out of someone's face	Stop harassing or annoying someone
Have the (brass) face to	Have the effrontery to do something
In your face	Aggressively obvious; assertive
Let's face it	Let's be honest, admitting unpalatable facts
Lose face	Suffer a loss or respect; be humiliated
On the face of it	Without necessarily knowing all of the relevant fact; at first glance
Put a brave (or bold or good) face on something	Act as if something unpleasant or upsetting is not as bad as it really is
Save face	Retain respect; avoid humiliation
Someone's face fits	Someone has the necessary qualities for something
Throw something back in someone's face	Reject something in a brusque or ungracious manner

A fact of life	Something that must be accepted and cannot be changed, however unpalatable
Do a fade	Run away
Without fail	Absolutely predictably; with no exception or cause for doubt
A faint heart	Timidity or lack of willpower preventing you from achieving your objective
Fair and square	Honestly and straight forwardly
A fair field and no favour	Equal conditions in a contest
Fair play to someone	Used as an expression of approval when someone has done something praiseworthy or the right thing under the circumstances
Fair's fair	Used to request just treatment or assert that an arrangement is just
Fairies (away) with the	Giving the impression of being mad, distracted, or in a dream world
Fall off (the back of) a lorry	Be acquired in illegal or unspecified circumstances (of goods)
Fall (or land) on your feet	Achieve a fortunate outcome to a difficult situation
Fall over yourself	Be excessively eager (to do something)
Take the fall	Receive blame or punishment, typically in the place of another person
A false dawn	A misleadingly hopeful sign

Sell the family silver	Part with a valuable resource in order to gain an immediate advantage
Famous for being famous	Having no recognizable reason for your fame other than high media exposure
Famous for fifteen minutes	Enjoying a brief period of fame before fading back into obscurity (especially of an ordinary person)
Fancy your (or someone's) chance	Believe that you (or someone else) are likely to be successful
Be a far cry from	Be very different from
Far and away	By a very large amount
So far, so good	Progress has been satisfactory up to now
To a fare-thee-well	To perfection; thoroughly
Like (or as if) it is going out of fashion (or style)	In great quantities and without restraint
Fast and furious	Lively and exciting
Play fast and loose	Ignore your obligations; be unreliable
In the fast lane	Where life is exciting or highly pressured
Pull a fast one	Try to gain an unfair advantage by rapid action of some sort

The fat is in the fire	Something has been said or done that is about to cause trouble or anger
Live off (or on) the fat of the land	Have the best of everything
A fate worse than death	A terrible experience, especially that of seduction or rape
Like father, like son	A son's character or behaviour can be expected to resemble that of his father
Kill the fatted calf	Produce a lavish celebratory feast
Do someone a favour	Do something for someone as an act of kindness
Favourite son	A famous man who is particularly popular and praised for his achievements in his native area
Put the fear of god in (or into) someone	Cause someone to be very frightened
Without fear or favour	Not influenced by any consideration of the people involved in a situation; impartially
Feast your eyes on	Gaze at with pleasure
Feast of famine	Either too much of something or too little
A ghost (or spectre) at the feast	Someone or something that brings glooms or sadness to an otherwise pleasant or celebratory occasion

A movable feast	An event which takes place at no regular time
A feather in your cap	An achievement to be proud of
Feather your (own) nest	Make money, usually illicitly and at someone else's expense
In find (or high) feather	In good spirits
Fed up to the teeth (or back teeth)	Extremely annoyed
Feel your age	Become aware that you are growing older and less energetic
In (or at) one fell swoop	All in one go
Over the fence	Unreasonable or unacceptable
Sit on the fence	Avoid making a decision or choice
Fetch and carry	Go backwards and forwards bringing things to someone in servile fashion
In fine fettle	In very good condition
Few and far between	Scarce or infrequent
Have a few	Drink enough alcohol to be slightly drunk
Fiddle while Rome burns	Be concerned with relatively trivial matters while ignoring the serious or disastrous events going on around you
Hang up your fiddle	Retire from business; give up an undertaking

Hang up your fiddle when you come home	Cease to be cheerful or entertaining when you are in the company of your family
Play second fiddle to	Take a subordinate role to someone or something
Have a field day	Have full scope for action, success, or excitement, especially at the expense of others
Fifth column	An organized group of people sympathizing with and working for the enemy within a country at war or otherwise under attack
In full fig	Wearing the smart clothes appropriate for an event or occasion
Fight fire with fire	Use the weapons on tactics of your enemy or opponent, even if you find them distasteful
Fight or flight	The instinctive physiological response to a threatening situation, which readies you either to resist violently or to run away
Fight shy of	Be unwilling to undertake or become involved with
Figure of fun	A person who is considered ridiculous
Have had your fill of	Have had as much or many of something as you want or can bear
Find your feet	Establish yourself in a particular situation or enterprise

Find it in your heart to do something	Allow or force yourself to do something
Fine feathers	Beautiful clothes
Not to put too fine a point on it	To speak bluntly
One fine day	At some unspecified or unknown time
The finer points of	The more complex or detailed aspects of
Your finest hour	The time of your greatest success
With a fine-tooth comb	Extremely thorough and detailed (of examination or analysis)
Be all finger and thumbs	Be clumsy or awkward in your actions
Burn your fingers (or get your fingers burned/burnt)	Suffer unpleasant consequences as a result of your actions
Have a finger in every pie	Be involved in large and varied number of activities or enterprises
Have a finger in the pie	Be involved in a matter, especially in an annoyingly interfering way
Have (or keep) your finger on the pulse	Be aware of all the latest news or development
Your fingers itch	You are longing or impatient to do something

At your fingertips	Readily available (especially of information)
A fight to the finish	A fight, contest, or match which only ends with the complete defeat of one of the parties involved
Breathe fire	Be fiercely angry
Under fire	Being rigorously criticized
Firing on all (four) cylinders	Working or functioning at a peak level
In the firing line	In a situation where you are subject to criticism or blame because of your responsibilities or position
Be on firm ground	Be sure of your facts or secure in your position, especially in a discussion
At first hand	Directly or from personal experience
First come, first served	Used to indicate that people will be dealt with strictly in the order in which they arrive or apply
First thing	Early in the morning; before anything else
First things first	Important matters should be attended to before anything else
A big fish in a small (or little) pond	A person seen as important and influential only within the limited scope of a small organization or group
Fish in troubled waters	Make a profit out of trouble or upheaval

A fish out of water	A person who is in a completely unsuitable environment or situation
Have other (or bigger) fish to fry	Have other or more important matters to attend to
Like shooting fish in a barrel	Done very easily
There are plenty more fish in the sea	Used to console someone whose romantic relationship has ended by pointing out that there are many other people with whom they may have a successful relationship in the future
Give someone a fit	Greatly shock, frighten, or anger someone
In fits	In a state of hysterical amusement
In (or by) fits and starts	With irregular bursts of activity
Five – finger discount	An act of shoplifting
Give someone five	Slap someone's palm as a gesture of celebration or greeting
Take five	Take a short break; relax
Flash in the pan	A thing or person whose sudden but brief success in not repeated or repeatable
Quick as a flash	Happening or made very quickly (especially of a person's response or reaction)
Fall flat	Fail completely to produce the intended or expected effect

Fall flat on your face	Fail in an embarrassingly obvious way
Flat out	1. As fast or as hard as possible 2. Without hesitation or reservation
Catch someone flat-footed	Take someone by surprise or at a disadvantage
Flavour of the month	Someone or something that enjoys a short period of great popularity; the current fashion
In the flesh	In person rather than via a telephone, film, article, etc.
Your (own) flesh and blood	Near relatives; close family
Flex your muscles	Give a show of strength or power
Flexible friend	A credit card
Give someone the flick (or get the flick)	Reject someone (or be rejected) in a casual or offhand way
In full flight	Escaping as rapidly as possible
Flog a dead horse	Waste energy on a lost cause or unalterable situation
Open the floodgates	Remove the last restraint holding back an outpouring of something powerful or substantial
From the floor	Delivered by an individual member at a meeting or assembly, rather than by a representative on the platform (of a speech or question)

Take the floor	1. Begin to dance on a dance floor
	2. Speak in a debate or assembly
Flotsam and jetsam	Useless or discarded objects
Go with the flow	Be relaxed; accept a situation
In the first flush	In a state of freshness and vigour
Flutter your eyelashes	Open and close your eyes rapidly in a coyly flirtatious manner
Die (or drop) like flies	Die or collapse in large numbers
Drink with the flies	Alone
Fly the coop	Make your escape
Fly high	Be very successful; prosper
A fly in amber	A curious relic of the past preserved into the present
A fly in the ointment	A minor irritation or other factor that spoils the success or enjoyment of something
Fly a kite	Try something out to test opinion
Fly the nest	Leave their parent's home to set up home elsewhere (of a young person)
Fly off the handle	Lose your temper suddenly and unexpectedly
A fly on the wall	An unnoticed observer of a particular situation
A fly on the wheel	A person who overestimates their own influence

With flying colours	With distinction
Follow suit	Conform to another's action
Food for thought	Something that warrants serious consideration or reflection
Be no (or nobody's) fool	Be a shrewd or prudent person
You could have fooled me!	Used to express cynicism or doubt about an assertion
Get your feet under the table	Establish yourself securely in a new situation
Get your feet wet	Begin to participate in an activity
Have feet of clay	Have a fatal flaw in a character that is otherwise powerful or admirable
Have a foot in both camps	Have an interest or stake in two parties or sides without commitment to either
Have (or get) a foot in the door	Have (or gain) a first introduction to a profession or organization
Have one foot in the grave	Be bear death through old age or illness
Have (or keep) your feet on the ground	Be (or remain) practical and sensible
Put your best foot forward	Embark on an undertaking with as much speed, effort, and determination as possible
Put your feet up	Take a rest, especially when reclining with your feet raised and supported

Put your foot down	Adopt a firm policy when faced with opposition or disobedience
Put a foot wrong	Make any mistake in performing an action
Footloose and fancy-free	Without any commitment or responsibilities; free to act or travel as you please
Play footsie with someone	Touch someone's feet lightly with your own feet, usually under a table, as a playful expression of romantic interest
Follow (or tread) in someone's footsteps	Do as another person did before, especially in making a journey or follow an occupation
Forbidden fruit	A thing that is desired all the more because it is not allowed
Force the issue	Compel the making of an immediate decision
In force	In great strength or numbers
With forked tongue	Untruthfully or deceitfully
A forlorn hope	A faint remaining hope or chance; a desperate attempt
Forty winks	A short sleep or nap, especially during the day
Foul your own nest	Do something damaging or harmful to yourself or your own interests
Founding father	Someone who establishes an institution

The fourth estate	The press; the profession of journalism
Frankenstein's monster	A thing that becomes terrifying or destructive to its maker
Free, gratis, and for nothing	Without charge
A free hand	Freedom to act at your own discretion
Walk free	Be released from custody having been exonerated
Freeze your blood	Fill you feelings of fear or horror
Excuse (or pardon) my French	Used to apologize for swearing
Take French leave	Make an unannounced or unauthorized departure
A fair- weather friend	Someone who cannot be relied on in a crisis
Friends in high places	People in senior positions who are able and willing to use their influence on your behalf
Have a frog in your throat	Lose your voice or find it hard to speak because of hoarseness or an apparent impediment in your throat
Front of house	The parts of a theatre in front of the proscenium arch
It'll be a frosty Friday (in July)	Used to indicate that something is very unlikely to happen

The game is up	The plan, deception, or crime is revealed or foiled
Game over	Said when a situation is regarded as hopeless or irreversible
Play games	Deal with someone or something in a way that lacks due seriousness or respect or deviates from the truth
Play someone's game	Advance another's plans, whether intentionally or not
Run the gamut	Experience, display, or perform the complete range of something
Go gangbusters	Proceed very vigorously or successfully game
Garbage in, garbage out	Incorrect or poor quality input inevitably produces faulty output
Everything in the garden is lovely (or rosy)	All is well
Lead someone up the garden path	Give someone misleading clues or signals
Step on the gas	Press on the accelerator to make a car go faster
Get (or be given) the gate	Be dismissed from a job
Run the gauntlet	Go through an intimidating or dangerous crowd, place, or experience in order to reach a goal

Throw down (or take up) the gauntlet	Issue (or accept) a challenge
Change gear	Begin to move or act differently, usually more rapidly
Give someone the gears	Harass or pester someone
A gentleman's agreement	An arrangement or understanding which is based on the trust of both or all parties, rather than being legally binding
Let George do it	Let someone else do the work or take the responsibility
The gift of the gab	The ability to speak with eloquence and fluency
Gild the lily	Try to improve what is already beautiful or excellent
Take the gilt off the gingerbread	Make something no longer appealing
Ginger group	A highly active faction within a party or movement that presses for stronger action on a particular issue
Gird (up) your loins	Prepare and strengthen yourself for what is to come
Don't give me that!	Don't ask me to believe that!(used as an expression of annoyed incredulity)
Give someone the glad hand	Offer someone a warm and hearty, but often insincere, greeting or welcome

Golden boy	A very popular or successful man
A golden handshake	A sum of money paid by an employer to a retiring or redundant employee
The golden mean	The avoidance of extremes
Golden oldie	An old song or film that is still well know and popular
Goldfish bowl	A place or situation lacking privacy
Never had it so good	Have never before enjoyed such prosperity
All someone's geese are swans	Someone habitually exaggerates the merits of undistinguished people or things
Kill the goose that lays the golden egg(s)	Destroy a reliable and valuable source of income
Play gooseberry	Be a third person who stays in the company of two people, especially lovers, who would prefer to be on their own
The gory details	The explicit details of something
Gospel truth	The absolute truth
Up for grabs	Available; obtainable
A grain of mustard seed	A small thing capable of vast development
A (or the) grand old man of	A man long and highly respected in a particular field

The green-eyed monster	Jealousy
Have green fingers	Have a natural ability to grow plants successfully
A grey area	An ill-defined situation or field not readily conforming to a category or to an existing set of rules
Little grey cells	Brain cells (as symbolic of high intelligence or mental acuity)
Grin and bear it	Suffer pain or misfortune in a stoical manner
Grind to a halt (or come to a grinding halt)	Move more and more slowly and them stop
Keep your nose to the grindstone	Work hard and continuously
Grist to the mill	Experience, material, or knowledge which can be turned to good use
Grit your teeth	Make a great effort to keep your resolve when faced with an unpleasant or painful duty
Grody to the max	Unspeakable awful
By the gross	In large numbers or amounts
Break new (or fresh) ground	Do something innovative which is considered and advance or positive benefit
Cut the ground from under someone's feet	Do something which leaves someone without a reason or justification for their actions or opinions

Get in on the ground floor	Become part of an enterprise in its early stages
On your own ground	On your own territory or concerning your own range of knowledge or experience
Prepare the ground	Make it easier for something to occur or be developed
Work (on run) yourself into the ground	Exhaust yourself by working or running very hard
Anyone's guess	A totally unpredictable matter
Your guess is as good as mine	I know as little about the matter as you (used in answer to a question)
Be my guest	Please do
Go great guns	Perform forcefully, vigorously, or successfully
Stick to your guns	Refuse to compromise or change, despite criticism
Top gun	A (or the) most important person
Under the gun	Under great pressure
Hack it	Manage; cope – usually used in the negative
Make someone's hackles rise	Make someone angry or indignant
Hail-fellow-well-met	Showing excessive familiarity
Hair of the dog	A small quantity of alcohol taken as remedy for a hangover
Half a chance	The slightest opportunity

Hamlet without the prince	A performance or event taking place without the principal actor
Come (or **go**) **under the hammer**	Be sold at an auction
Hammer and tongs	With great energy and noise
Bind (or **tie**) **someone hand and foot**	Severely restrict someone's freedom to act or make decisions
Do something with one hand (tied) behind your back	Do something easily
Hand in glove	Close collusion or association
Hands off!	Used to warn someone against touching or interfering with something
Put your hands up	Raise your hands in surrender or to signify assent or participation
The right hand doesn't know what the left hand's doing	There is a state of confusion or a failure of communication within a group organization
Take someone or something in hand	Take someone or something under your control especially in order to improve them
Turn your hand to something	Undertake an activity different from your usual occupation

Make a hash of	Make a mess of; bungle
Pass the hat round	Collect contributions of money from a number of people for a specific purpose
Pull one out of the hat	Bring off an unexpected trick in an apparently desperate situation
Throw your hat in (or into) the ring	Indicate willingness to take up a challenge or enter a contest
Down the hatch	Used to express friendly feelings towards your companions before drinking
Hatches, matches, and dispatches	The births, marriage, and deaths columns in a newspaper
Have it out with someone	Attempt to resolve a contentious matter by confronting someone and engaging in a frank discussion or argument
Make hay	Make good use of an opportunity while it lasts
Above your head	Beyond your ability to understand
Bite (or snap) someone's head off	Reply sharply and brusquely to someone
Come (or bring) to a head	Reach (or cause to reach) a crisis
Do something standing on your head	Do something very easily

Have your heart in the right place	Be sincere or well intentioned
Heart and soul	Great energy and enthusiasm
Heart of gold	A generous nature
Heart of stone	A stern or cruel nature
Heart to heart	Candidly or intimately
In your heart of hearts	In your innermost feelings
Take something to heart	Take something seriously; be much affected or upset by something
Wear your heart on your sleeve	Make your feelings apparent
Your heart's desire	Someone or something that is greatly wished for
A heartbeat (away) from	Very close to; on the verge of
Hearth and home	Home and its comforts
In the heat of the moment	While temporarily angry, excited, or engrossed, and without stopping for thought
In seventh heaven	In a state of ecstasy
The heavens opened	It started to rain suddenly and very heavily
Take to your heels (or legs)	Run away

All hell broke (or was let) loose	Suddenly there was chaos or uproar,
Come hell or high water	No matter what difficulties may occur
For the hell of it	Just for fun
Get the hell out (of)	Escape from a place or situation very quickly
Give someone (or get) hell	Reprimand someone (or be reprimanded) severely
So help me (God)	Used to emphasize that you mean what you are saying
Rare (or scarce) as hen's teeth	Extremely rare
Here today, gone tomorrow	Soon over or forgotten; short-lived or transient
Neither here nor there	Of no importance or relevance
Hide your light under a bushel	Keep quiet about your talents or accomplishments
High and dry	In a difficult position, especially without resources
High days and holidays	Special occasions
Hit the high spots	Visit places of entertainment
On a high	In a state of euphoria

Ancient (or old) as the hills	Of very long standing or very great age
In someone's hip pocket	Completely under someone's control
Hire and fire	Engage and dismiss
Be history	Be perceived as no longer
Make history	Do something that is remembered in or influences the course of history
Hit and miss	Done or occurring at random; succeeding by chance rather than through planning
Hit the mark	Be successful in an attempt or accurate in a guess
Hit the nail on the head	State the truth exactly; find exactly the right answer
Hitch your wagon to a star	Make use of powers higher than your own
Play (or raise) hob	Cause mischief; make a fuss
Go the whole hog	Do something completely or thoroughly
Hold the fort	Take responsibility for a situation while someone is absent
Hold (or put) a gun (or a pistol) to someone's head	Force someone to do something by using threats
Hold your thumbs	Fold your fingers over your thumbs to bring good luck; hope for luck or success

An honest broker	A disinterested intermediary or mediator
By hook or by crook	By one means or another; by fair means or foul
Play hockey	Stay away from school without permission or explanation; play truant
Hope against hope	Cling to a mere possibility
Make a Horlicks of	Make a mess of
Blow (or toot) your own horn	Talk boastfully about yourself or your achievements
On the horn	On the telephone
On the horns of a dilemma	Faced with a decision involving equally unfavourable alternatives
A hornets' nest	A situation fraught with trouble, opposition, or complications
Straight from the horse's mouth	From the person directly concerned or another authoritative source
A horse of another (or different) colour	A thing significantly different
Go hot and cold	Experience sudden feelings of fear, embarrassment, or shock
Hot air	Empty talk that is intended to impress
Hot to trot	Ready and eager to engage in an activity

Hot under the collar	Angry, resentful, or embarrassed
In hot water	In a situation of difficulty, trouble, or disgrace
Keep late (or regular) hours	Do the same thing, typically getting up and going to bed, late (or at the same time) everyday
Get on (or along) like a house on fire	Have a very good and friendly relationship
A house divided	A group or organization weakened by internal dissensions
A house of cards	An insecure or overambitious scheme
Put (or set or get) your house in order	Make necessary reforms
And how!	Very much so (used to express strong agreement)
Huff and puff	Breathe heavily with exhaustion
Hum and haw (or ha)	Hesitate; be indecisive
Live on your hump	Be self-sufficient
Break the ice	Do or say something to relieve tension or get conversation started at the start of a party
Skating on thin ice	In a precarious or risky situation

An iron hand (or fist) in a velvet glove	Firmness or ruthlessness masked by outward gentleness
Iron out the wrinkles	Resolve all minor difficulties and snags
An itching palm	An avaricious or greedy nature
Before you can say Jack Robinson	Very quickly or suddenly
Every man Jack	Each and every person
On your Jack	On your own
Plain Jane	An unattractive girl or woman
The jewel in the (or someone's) crown	The most attractive or successful part of something
In jig time	Extremely quickly; in a very short time
The whole jingbang	The whole lot
A Job's comforter	A person who aggravates distress under the guise of giving comfort
Do a job on someone	Do something which harms or defeats an opponent
Just the job	Exactly what is needed
More than your job's worth	Not worth risking your job for

You can't keep a good man (or woman) down	A competent person will always recover well from setbacks or problems
Beyond your ken	Outside your range of knowledge or understanding
A different kettle of fish	A completely different matter or type of person from the one previously mentioned
Put the kibosh on	Put an end to; thwart the plans of
Kick the bucket	Die
Kick someone down the ladder	Reject or disown the friends or associates who have helped you to rise in the world, especially with the idea of preventing them from attaining a similar position
Kick the gong around	Smoke opium
Kick the habit	Stop engaging in a habitual practice
A kick in the teeth	A grave setback or disappointment, especially one seen as a betrayal
Kick the tin	Make a contribution of money for a particular purpose
Kick someone upstairs	Remove someone from an influential position in a business by giving them an ostensible promotion
Kick someone when they are down	Cause future misfortune to someone who is already in a difficult situation

Kill time	Do things to make time seem to pass more quickly and to avoid getting bored, especially while waiting for something
Make a killing	Have a great financial success, especially on a stock exchange
Out of kilter	Out of harmony or balance
King or Kaiser	Any powerful earthly ruler
A king's ransom	A huge amount of money; a fortune
Till (or until) kingdom come	Forever
Kiss and make up	Become reconciled
Kiss and tell	Recount your sexual exploits, especially to the media concerning a famous person
Kiss of death	An action or event that causes certain failure for an enterprise
Kiss the dust	Submit abjectly; be overthrown
Kiss the ground	Prostrate yourself as a token of respect
Kiss the rod	Accept punishment meekly or submissively
Kiss something goodbye (or kiss goodbye to something)	Accept the certain loss of something
High as kite	Intoxicated with drugs or alcohol

Kith and kin	Your relations
Bring someone or something to their knees	Reduce someone or something to a state of weakness or submission
Weak at the knees	Overcome by a strong emotion
Your knees are knocking	You are feeling very frightened
Ring the knell of	Announce or herald the end of
Before you can say jack knife	Very quickly; almost instantaneously
Go (or be) under the knife	Very surgery
Like a (hot) knife through butter	Very easily; without any resistance or difficulty
The knives are out (for someone)	There is open hostility (towards someone)
On a knife-edge (or razor's edge)	In a tense situation, especially one finely balanced between success and failure
A knight in shining armour	An idealized or heroic person, especially a man who comes to the rescue of a woman in distress or in a difficult situation
Knock some-one's block off	Hit someone very hard in anger

Knock someone dead	Greatly impress someone
Knock someone into the middle of next week	Hit someone very hard
Knock someone or something on the head	Decisively prevent an idea, or developed
Knock spots off	Easily outdo
Take a knock	Suffer a material or emotional setback
On the Knocker	Going from door to door, usually canvassing, buying or selling
Tie someone (up) in knots	Make someone completely confused
As we know it	As is familiar or customary in the present
Know better than	Be wise, well-informed, or well-mannered enough to avoid doing something specified
Know the score	Be aware of what is going on; be aware of the essential facts about a situation
Know too much	Be in possession of too much important information to be allowed to live or continue as normal
Know what's what	Have enough knowledge or experience
Know who's who	Be aware of the identity and status of each person

Speak the same language	Understand one another as a result of shared opinions and values
Fall (or drop) into someone's lap	Come someone's way without any effort having been made
In the lap of luxury	In conditions of great comfort and wealth
Be the last word	Be the most fashionable or up-to-date
Drinking in the last chance saloon	Having been allowed one final opportunity to improve or get something right
Last but not least	Last in order of mention or occurrence but not of importance
Last hurrah	A final act, performance, or efforts especially in politics
The last of the Mohicans	The sole survivor(s) of a particular race of kind
Late in the day	At a late stage in proceedings, especially too late to be useful
Don't make me laugh	Don't say such ridiculous things
Good for a laugh	Guaranteed to amuse or entertain
Have the last laugh	Be finally vindicated, thereby confounding earlier scepticism
Laugh all the way to the bank	Make a great deal of money with very little effort

Laugh in someone's face	Show open contempt for someone by laughing rudely at them in their presence
Laugh like a drain	Laugh raucously; guffaw
A laugh a minute	Very funny
Laugh on the other side of your face	Be discomfited after feeling satisfaction or confidence about something
Laugh someone or something to scorn	Ridicule someone or something
Be laughing	Be in a fortunate or comfortable situation
Laughing stock	A person subjected to general mockery or ridicule
Look to your laurels	Be careful not to lose your superior position to a rival
Rest on your laurels	Be so satisfied with what you have already done or achieved that you make no further effort
Be a law unto yourself	Behave in a manner that is not conventional or predictable
Lay down the law	Issue instructions to other people in an authoritative or dogmatic way
Take the law into your hands	Punish someone for an offence according to your own ideas of justice, especially in an illegal or violent way

Lay a charge	Make an accusation
Lay something to rest	Soothe and dispel fear, anxiety, grief, and similar unpleasant emotions
Lay something up in lavender	Preserve something carefully for future use
Get the lead out	Move or work more quickly; hurry up
Go down (or over) like a lead balloon	Fail; be a flop
Lead someone by the nose	Control someone totally, especially by deceiving them
Lead from the front	Take an active role in what you are urging and directing others to do
Lead with your chin	Behave or speak incautiously
Shake (or tremble) like a leaf	Tremble greatly, especially from fear
Take a leaf out of someone's book	Closely imitate or emulate someone in a particular way
Turn over a new leaf	Improve your conduct or performance
A leap in the dark	A daring step or enterprise whose consequences are unpredictable
A new lease of (or on) life	A substantially improved prospect of life or use after rejuvenation or repair

To say the least (or the least it)	Used as an understatement or euphemism to imply that the reality is more extreme, usually worse
Leave someone cold	Fail to interest or excite someone
Like a leech	Persistently or clingingly present
Make up (the) leeway	Struggle out of a bad position, especially by recovering lost time
Be left at the post	Fail to complete
Left-handed compliment	A remark that is superficially complimentary but contains a strong element of adverse criticism
On your hind legs	Standing up to make a speech
On your last legs	Near the end of life
A legend in their own lifetime	A very famous or notorious person
Go legit	Begin to behave honestly after a period of illegal activity
Lady (or man or gentleman) of leisure	A person who does not need to earn a living or whose time is free from obligations to others
The answer's a lemon	The response or outcome is unsatisfactory
Hand someone a lemon	Pass off a substandard article as good; swindle someone

Lend your name to something	Allow yourself to be publicly associated with something
Lenten fare	Meagre rations that do not include meat
A leopard can't change his spots	People can't change basic nature
In less than no time	Very quickly or soon
Let or hindrance	Obstruction or impediment
A man (or woman) of letters	A scholar or writer
To the letter	With adherence to every detail
Do your level best	Do your utmost; make all possible efforts
A level playing field	A situation in which everyone has a fair and equal chance of succeeding
Take liberties	Behave in an unduly familiar manner towards a person
Licence to print money	A very lucrative commercial activity, typically one perceived as requiring little effort
A lick and a promise	A hasty performance of a task, especially of cleaning something
Blow the lid off	Remove means of restraint and allow something to get out of control

The bottom line	The final reality; the important conclusion
Come down to the line	Be closely fought right until the end (of a race)
The lion's den	A demanding, intimidating, or unpleasant place or situation
The lion's mouth	A place of great peril
Throw someone to the lions	Cause someone to be in an extremely dangerous or unpleasant situation
Bite your lip	Repress an emotion; stifle laughter or a retort
Curl your lip	Raise a corner of your upper lip to show contempt; sneer
Hang on someone's lips	Listen attentively to someone
Pay lip service to something	Express approval of or support for something without taking any significant action
Liquid lunch	A drinking session at lunchtime taking the place of a meal
Enter the lists	Issue or accept a challenge
Little stranger	A newly born baby
Live and breathe something	Be extremely interested in or enthusiastic about a particular subject or activity
Live out of a suitcase	A great deal of travelling
Live your own life	Follow your own plans and principles; be independent of others

Live rough	Live and sleep outdoors as a consequence of having no proper home
Live to fight another day	Survive a certain experience or ordeal
Live to tell the tale	Survive a dangerous experience and be able to tell others about it
Live wire	An energetic and unpredictable person
Get a load of	Used to draw attention to someone or something
Get (or have) a load on	Become drunk
Have a lock on	Have an unbreakable hold or total control over
Lock horns	Engage in conflict
At loggerheads	In violent dispute or disagreement
Loiter with intent	Stand or wait around with the intention of committing an offence
Lone wolf	A person who prefers to act alone
The long and the short of it	All that can or need be said
Long home	Death
Long in the tooth	Rather old
Draw the longbow	Make exaggerated claims or statements
Look someone in the eye (or face)	Look directly at someone without showing embarrassment, fear, or shame

Look someone up and down	Scrutinize someone carefully
Look the other way	Deliberately ignore wrongdoing by others
Look sharp	Be quick
Be on the lookout	Keep searching for someone or something that is wanted
Throw (or knock) someone for a loop	Surprise or astonish someone; catch someone off guard
A loose cannon	An unpredictable person or thing likely to cause unintentional damage
At a loose end	Having nothing to do; not knowing what to do
Lose your (or the) way	No longer have a clean idea of your purpose or motivation in an activity or business
All is not lost	Used to suggest that there is still some chance of success or recovery
Be lost on someone	Fail to influence or be noticed or appreciated by someone
Give someone up for lost	Stop expecting that a missing person will be found alive
Make up for lost time	Do something faster or more often in order to compensate for not having done it quickly or often enough before
Throw in your lot with	Decide to ally yourself closely with and share the fate of a person or group

Love me, love my dog	If you love someone, you must accept everything about them, even their faults
Not for love or money	Not in any circumstances
The lowest of the low	Those regarded as the most immoral or socially inferior off all
A lump in the throat	A feeling of tightness or dryness in the throat caused by strong emotion, especially grief
Take (or get) your lumps	Suffer punishment; be attacked or defeated
There's no such thing as a free lunch	You never get something for nothing; any benefit received has eventually to be paid for
Leave someone in the lurch	Leave an associate or friend abruptly and without assistance or support when they are in a difficult situation
Take something lying down	Accept an insult or injury without attempting retaliation
Wax lyrical about (or over)	Talk in an effusive or enthusiastic way about something
Mad as a hatter (or a March hare)	Completely crazy
Far from the madding crowd	Secluded or removed from public notice
What you are made of	Your true abilities or qualities

Wave a (or your) magic wand	Exercise an arbitrary (quasisupernatural) power in order to make something happen
By main force	Through sheer strength
Make someone's day	Make an otherwise ordinary or dull day pleasingly memorable for someone
Meet your maker	Die
Man and boy	Throughout life from youth
A man for all seasons	A man who is ready to cope with any contingency and whose behaviour is always appropriate to every occasion
The man in (or on) the street	An ordinary person, usually with regard to their opinions, or as distinct from an expert
Man of the moment	A man of importance at a particular time
Man of straw	A person compared to an effigy stuffed with straw; a sham
A man's man	A man whose personality is such that he is more popular and at ease with other men than with women
Man to man	In a direct and frank way between two men; openly and honestly
Men in (grey) suits	Powerful men within an organization who exercise their influence or authority anonymously

Mark someone's card	Give someone information
The mark of Cain	The stigma of a murderer; a sign of infamy
Mark time	Pass your time in routine activities until a more interesting opportunity presents itself
Marriage of convenience	A marriage concluded to a achieve a practical purpose
To the marrow	To your innermost being
Marry money	Marry a rich person
Go to the mat	Vigorously engage in an argument or dispute, typically on behalf of a particular person or cause
Meet your match	Encounter your equal in strength or ability
Do the math!	Work it out for yourself
Waltz (or walk) Matilda	Carry a bundle of your personal possessions as you travel the roads
Make a meal of	Treat a task or occurrence with more attention or care than necessary, especially for effect
Mean business	Be in earnest
A means to an end	A thing that is not valued or important in itself but is useful in achieving an aim
For good measure	In addition to what has already been done, said, or given
Measure your length	Fall flat on the ground (of a person)

Be meat and drink to	Be a source of great pleasure or encouragement to
A dose (or taste) of your own medicine	The same bad treatment that you have given to others
Meek as Moses (or a lamb)	Very meek
A meeting of minds	An understanding or agreement between people
Melt in the mouth	Be deliciously light or tender and need little or no chewing (of food)
Mend (your) fences	Make peace with a person
Be mentioned in dispatches	Be commended for your actions
The more the merrier	The more people or things there are the better a situation will be
Mess with someone's head	Cause someone to feel frustrated, anxious, or upset
Get the message	Infer an implication from a remark or action
Send the right (or wrong) message	Make a significant, either implicitly or by your actions
Shoot (or kill) the messenger	Treat the bearer of bad news as if they were to blame for it
Be on your mettle	Be ready or forced to prove your ability to copy well with a demanding situation

Put someone on their mettle	Test someone's ability to face difficulties in a spirited and resilient way
Take the mickey	Tease or ridicule someone, especially in an unkind or persistent way
Slip someone a Mickey Finn	Give someone a drugged or otherwise adulterated drink
Under the microscope	Under critical examination
The Midas touch	The ability to make money out of anything that you undertake
The middle of nowhere	Somewhere very remote and isolated
Might is right	Those who are powerful can do what they wish unchallenged
Be miles away	Be lost in thought and so unaware of what is happening around you
Go the extra mile	Be especially assiduous in your attempt to achieve something
A mile a minute	Very quickly
Run a mile	Used to show that someone is frightened by or very unwilling to do something
Cry over spilt (or spilled) milk	Lament or make a fuss about a misfortune that has happened and that cannot be changed or reversed
The milk of human kindness	Care and compassion for others
A – in a million	One of the very best of their kind

A millstone round you neck	A very severe impediment or disadvantage
Not mince words (or matters)	Speak candidly and directly, especially when criticizing someone or something
Make mincemeat of	Defeat decisively or easily in a fight, contest, or argument
Great minds think alike	Used to flag up the coincidence when two people think of the same thing at the same time or have the same opinion
In your mind's eye	In your imagination or mental view
Mind your Ps and Qs	Be careful to behave well and avoid giving offence
Mind the shop	Be temporarily in charge of affairs
Mind your back (or backs)	Used to warn inattentive bystanders that someone wants to get past
Never mind	Used to urge someone not to feel anxiety or distress
Not pay someone any mind	Not pay someone any attention
On someone's mind	Preoccupying someone, especially in a disquieting way
Open your mind to	Be prepared to consider or acknowledge; be receptive to
Out of your mind	Having lost control of your mental faculties; insane
In a minor key	Understated (especially of a literary work)

In mint condition	New or as if new; in pristine condition (of an object)
One minute to midnight	The last moment or opportunity
All done with mirrors	Achieved with an element of trickery
Make mischief	Create trouble or discord
Make no mistake (about it)	Do not be deceived into thinking otherwise
Get your mitts on	Obtain possession of
Mix and match	Select and combine different but complementary items, such as clothing or pieces of equipment, to form a coordinated set
A mixed bag	A diverse assortment of things or people
A mixed blessing	Something good which nevertheless has some disadvantages
The mixture as before	The same treatment repeated
Put the mockers on	Put an end to; thwart
Make a mockery of something	Make something seem foolish or absurd
Moment of truth	A crisis; a turning point when a decision has to be made or a crisis faced

Monday morning quarterback	A person who is wise after the event
Have money to burn	Have so much money that you can spend as lavishly as you want
Money burns a hole in your pocket (or purse)	You have an irresistible urge to spend money as soon as you have it
Money talks	Wealth gives power and influence to those who possess it
Put money (or put your money) on	Have confidence in the truth or success of something
Put your money where your mouth is	Take action to support your statements or opinions
Throw money at something	Try to solve a problem by recklessly spending more money on it, without due consideration of what is required
Have a monkey on your back	Be dependent on drugs
I'll be a monkey's uncle	Used to express great surprise
Like a money on a stick	Restless and agitated
Put (or get) a person's monkey up	Make someone angry

A month of Sundays	A very long, seemingly endless period of time
The full monty	The full amount expected, desired, or possible
Bay at the moon	Clamour or make an outcry to no effect
Many moons ago	A long time ago
Over the moon	Extremely happy; delighted
Promise someone the moon (or earth)	Promise something that is unattainable
Do a moonlight flit	Make a hurried, usually nocturnal, removal or change of abode, especially in order to avoid paying your rent
Moonlight and roses	Used to characterize an atmosphere of romantic sentimentality
Morton's fork	A situation is which there are two choices or alternatives whose consequences are equally unpleasant
A mote in someone's eye	A trivial fault in someone which is less serious than one in someone else who is being critical
Wear motley	Play the fool
Have a mountain to climb	Be facing a very difficult task

Make a mountain out of a molehill	Foolishly or pointlessly exaggerate the importance of something trivial
Move mountains	Make every possible effort
Make someone's mouth water	Cause someone to salivate at the prospect of appetizing food
Put the mouth on someone	Cause someone's performance to deteriorate by praising it
Give someone a mouthful	Talk to or shout at someone in an angry, abusive, or severely critical way; swear at someone
Get a move on	Hurry up
Make a move	Take action
A mover and shaker	Someone at the centre of events who makes things happen; a powerful person
Much of a muchness	Very similar; nearly the same
Where there's muck there's brass	Dirty or unpleasant activities are also lucrative
Fling (or sling or throw) mud	Make disparaging or scandalous remark or accusation
Here's mud in your eye	Used to express friendly feelings towards your companions before drinking

Muddy the waters	Make an issue or a situation more confusing and harder to understand by introducing complications
A mug's game	An activity which it is stupid to engage in because it is likely to be unsuccessful or dangerous
Mum's the word	Say nothing; don't reveal a secret
Murphy's law	If anything can go wrong it will
Like mushrooms	Suddenly and in great numbers
Mutton dressed as lamb	A middle-aged or old woman dressed in a style suitable for a much younger woman
A nail in the coffin	An action or event regarded as likely to have a detrimental or destructive effect on a situation, enterprise, or person
Nail a lie	Expose something as a falsehood or deception
On the nail	Without delay (of payment)
The naked truth	The plain truth, without concealment or embellishment
Call someone names	Insult someone verbally
Drop names	Refer frequently to well-known people in such a way as to imply that they are close acquaintances
Give your name to	Invent, discover, or found something which then becomes known by your name

In name only	By description but not in reality
Name and shame	Identify wrongdoers by name with the intention of embarrassing them into improving their behaviour
Name names	Mention specific names, especially of people involved in something wrong or illegal
Name no names	Refrain from mentioning the names of people involved in an incident
The name of the game	The main purpose or most important aspect of a situation
No names, no pack drill	Punishment or blame cannot be meted out if names and details are not mentioned
Put a name to	Know or manage to remember what someone or something is called
Something has your name on it	You are destined or particularly suited to receive or experience a specified thing
What's in a name?	Names are arbitrary labels
Catch someone napping	Find someone off guard and unprepared to respond
A nasty piece (or bit) of work	An unpleasant or untrustworthy person
One nation	A nation not divided by social inequality
In the nature of things	Inevitable or inevitably

Your better nature	The good side of your character; your capacity for tolerance, generosity, or sympathy
Naughty but nice	Reprehensible but irresistible
Your nearest and dearest	Your close friends and relatives
A necessary evil	Something that is undesirable but must be accepted
Break your neck to do something	Expert yourself to the utmost to achieve something
Neck and neck	Level in a race, competition, or comparison
Get the (dead) needle	Become very annoyed
A needle in a haystack	Something that is almost impossible to find because it is concealed by so many other similar things
Not on your nelly	Certainly not
Touch (or (hit) a (raw) nerve	Provoke a reaction by referring to a sensitive topic
Slip (or fall) through the net	Escape from or be missed by something organized to catch or deal with you
No news is good news	Without information to the contrary you can assume that all is well
A New York minute	A very short time; a moment

No more Mr Nice Guy	Used to suggest that you will stop being lenient and begin to adopt more severe measures
In the nick of time	Only just in time; just at the critical moment
Dressed (up) to the nines	Dressed very smartly or elaborately
No more than ninepence in the shilling	Of low intelligence
Nip something in the bud	Suppress or destroy something at an early stage
Nip and tuck	Very closely contested; neck and neck
No man's land	An intermediate or ambiguous area of thought or activity
Get (or give someone or something) the nod	Be selected or approved (or select or approve someone or something)
A nod's as good as a wink	There's no need for further elaboration or explanation
Nod the nut	Plead guilty to a charge in court
On the nod	By general agreement and without discussion
Be on nodding terms	Know someone slightly
A no-go area	An area which is dangerous or impossible to enter or to which entry is restricted or forbidden

Make nonsense (or a nonsense) of	Reduce the value of something to a ridiculous degree
Every nook and cranny	Every part or aspect or something
Put your head in a noose	Bring about your own downfall
By a nose	By a very narrow margin (of a victory)
Count noses	Count people, typically in order to determine the numbers in a vote
Cut off your nose to spite your face	Disadvantage yourself in the course of trying to disadvantage another
Get up someone's nose	Irritate or annoy someone
Give someone a bloody nose	Inflict a resounding defeat on someone
Have a nose for	Have an instinctive talent for detecting (something)
Keep your nose clean	Stay out of trouble
Keep your nose out of	Refrain from interfering in someone else's affairs
Put someone's nose out of joint	Upset or annoy someone
Turn up your nose at	Show distaste or contempt for something

With your nose in the air	Haughtily
Not in my back yard	Expressing an objection to the setting of something regarded as undesirable in your won neighbourhood, with the implication that it would be acceptable
Be as nothing (compared) to	Be insignificant in comparison with
Nothing doing	There is no prospect of success or agreement
At short (or a moment's) notice	With little warning or time for preparation
Put someone on notice (or serve notice)	Warn someone of something about or likely to occur, often in a formal or threatening way
To the nth degree	To any extent; to the utmost
Make your number	Report your arrival, pay a courtesy call, or report for duty
Without number	Too many to count
A wooden nutmeg	A false or fraudulent thing
In a nutshell	In the fewest possible words
Keep both oars in the water	Maintain a calm equilibrium in your life and affairs
Fell your oats	Feel lively and buoyant

Off your oats	Lacking an appetite
Sow your wild oats	Go through a period of wild or promiscuous behaviour while young
The object of the exercise	The main point or purpose of an activity
Odd one (or man) out	Someone or something that is different to the others
Ask no odds	Ask no favours
By all odds	Certainly
Odds and ends	Miscellaneous articles and remnants
Be in good (or bad) odour with someone	Be in (or out of) favour with someone
Good offices	Help and support, often given by exercising your influence
Just another day at the office	Boring routine
In the offing	Nearby; likely to happen or appear soon
Make old bones	Live to an advanced age
Of the old school	Traditional or old fashioned
Hold out (or offer) an olive branch	Offer a token of peace or goodwill
Be on to something	Be close to discovering the truth about an illegal or undesirable activity that someone is engaging in

Once and for all (or once for all)	Now and for the last time; finally
Once bitten, twice shy	A bad experience makes your wary of the same thing happening again
The one that got away	Something desirable that has eluded capture
One-horse race	A contest in which one candidate or competitor is clearly superior to all the others and seems certain to win
One-trick pony (or horse)	Someone or something specializing in only one area, having only one talent, or of limited ability
Know your onions	Be full knowledgeable about something
Be open with	Speak frankly to; conceal nothing from
In (or into) the open	Out of doors
The opium of the people (or masses)	Something regarded as inducing a false and unrealistic sense of contentment among people
Opportunity knocks	A chance of success occurs
Keep (or leave) our options open	Avoid committing yourself
Squeeze (or stuck) an orange	Take all that is profitable out of something

Get your own back	Take action in retaliation for a wrong-doing or insult
Change of pace	A change from what you are used to
Put someone or something through their paces	Make someone or something demonstrate their qualities or abilities
Stand (or stay) the pace	Be able to keep up with another or others
Pack your bag (or bags)	Put your belongings in a bag or suitcase in preparation for your imminent departure
Send someone packing	Make someone leave in an abrupt or peremptory way
Paddle your own canoe	Be independent and self-sufficient
Page three girl	A model whose nude or seminude photograph appears as part of a regular series in a tabloid newspaper
Put paid to	Stop abruptly; destroy
No pain, no gain	Suffering is necessary in order to achieve something
A pain in the neck	An annoying or tedious person or thing
Like watching paint dry	(of an activity or experience) extremely boring
I have only got one pair of hands	Used to deflect further demands for you to do work when you are already extremely busy

Pair of hands	A person seen in terms of their participation in a task
Beyond the pale	Outside the bounds of acceptable behaviour
Go down the pan	Reach a stage of abject failure or uselessness
A Pandora's box	A process that once begun generates many complicated problems
Press (or push or hit) the panic button	Respond to a situation by panicking or taking emergency measures
Make the papers	Be written about or given attention as news
Not worth the paper it is written on	Of no value or validity whatsoever (of an agreement, promise, etc.)
Paper over the cracks	Disguise problems or division rather than trying to solve them
A paper tiger	An apparently dangerous but actually ineffectual person or thing
Send in your papers	Resign
Above par	Better than average
At par	At face value
On a par with	Equal in importance or quality to; on an equal level with
Up to par	At an expected or usual level or quality
Be part and parcel of	Be an essential feature or element of

A (or the) parting of the ways	A point at which two people must separate or at which a decision must be taken
Party animal	A sociable person who enjoys parties
Make a pass it	Make an amorous or sexual advance to
Pass your sell-by date	Reach a point where you are useless or worn out
Pastures new (fresh field and)	A place or activity regarded as offering new opportunities
Put someone out to pasture	Force someone to retire
Not a patch on	Greatly inferior to
Give pause to someone (or give someone pause (for thought)	Cause someone to think carefully or hesitate before doing something
Pay the piper	Pay the cost of an enterprise
Pay your respects	Make a polite visit to someone
Pay through the nose	Pay much more than a fair price
Like peas (or like as two peas) in a pod	So similar as to be indistinguishable or nearly so
Hold your peace	Remain silent about something

Pick someone's brains (or brain)	Question someone who is better informed about a subject than yourself in order to obtain information
Pick something clean	Completely remove the flesh from a bone or carcass
Pick up the pieces	Restore your life or a situation to a more normal state, typically after a shock or disaster
Pick up the threads	Resume something that has been interrupted
Be no picnic	Be difficult or unpleasant
Get the picture	Understand a situation
Out of the picture	No longer involved; irrelevant
Nice (or sweet) as pie	Extremely nice or agreeable
Give someone a piece of your mind	Tell someone what you think, especially when you are angry about their behaviour
Go to pieces	Become so nervous or upset that you are unable to behave or perform normally
Say your piece	Give your opinion or a prepared statement
Bring (or drive) your pigs to market	Succeed in realizing your potential
In a pig's eye	Expressing scornful disbelief at a statement

Make a pig of yourself	Overeat
Make a pig's ear of	Bungle; make a mess of
On the pig's back	Living a life of ease and luxury; in a very fortunate situation
Pig (or piggy) in the middle	A person who is placed in an awkward situation between two others
A pig in a poke	Something that is bought or accepted without knowing its value or seeing it first
Sweet like a pig	Sweat profusely
Be someone's pigeon	Be someone's concern or affair
A bitter pill (to swallow)	An unpleasant or painful necessity (to accept)
Sugar (or sweeten) the pill	Make an unpleasant or painful necessity more acceptable
From pillar to post	From one place to another in an unceremonious or fruitless manner
A pillar of society	A person regarded as a particularly responsible citizen
Drop the pilot	Abandon a trustworthy adviser
On pins and needles	In an agitated state of suspense
You could hear a pin drop	There was absolute silence or stillness
At a pinch	If necessary; in an emergency

In the pink	In extremely good health and spirits
Give someone the pip	Make someone irritated or depressed
Pip someone at (or to) the post	Defeat someone at the last moment
In the pipeline	Being planned or developed; about to happen
Piping hot	Very hot
A pitched battle	A fierce fight
Place in the sun	A position of favour or advantage
Walk the plank	Lose your job or position
On a plate	With little or no effort from the person concerned
On your plate	Occupying your time or energy
Play a blinder	Perform very well
Play both ends against the middle	Keep your options open by supporting or favouring opposing sides
Play by the rules	Follow what is generally held to be the correct line of behaviour
Play fair	Observe principles of justice; avoid cheating
Play someone false	Prove treacherous or deceitful towards someone; let someone down
Play into someone's hands	Act in such a way as unintentionally to give someone an advantage
Play the market	Speculate in stocks
Sign (or take) the pledge	Make a solemn undertaking to abstain from alcohol

Plight your troth	Pledge your word in marriage or betrothal
Lose the plot	Lose your ability to understand what is happening; lose touch with reality
The plot thickens	The situation becomes more difficult and complex
Take the plunge	Commit yourself to a course of action about which you aare nervous
Plus – minus	More or less; roughly
Poacher turned gamekeeper	Someone who now protects the interests which they previously attacked
Have deep pockets	Have large financial resources
In someone's pocket	Dependent on someone financially and therefore under their influence
Live in someone's pocket	Live very close to someone and be closely involved with them
Out of pocket	Having lost money in a transaction
Pay out of pocket	Pay for something with your own money
Put your hand in your pocket	Spend or provide your own money
Poetic justice	The fact of experiencing a fitting or deserved retribution for your actions
A poisoned chalice	Something that is apparently desirable but likely to be damaging to the person to whom it is given
Poke your nose into	Take an intrusive interest in; pry into
Be poles apart	Differ greatly in nature or opinion

In pole position	In an advantageous position
Play politics	Act for political or personal gain rather than from principle
In your pomp	In your period of greatest effectiveness; in your prime
Poor as a church mouse (or as church mice)	Extremely poor
Poor little rich girl (or boy)	A wealthy young person whose money brings them no contentment (often used as an expression of mock sympathy)
Pop your clogs	Die
Is the pope (a) Catholic?	Used to indicate that something is blatantly obvious
Like someone possessed	Very violently or wildly, as if under the control of an evil spirit
Play possum	Pretend to be asleep or unconscious when threatened
Go postal	Go mad, especially from stress
Keep someone posted	Keep someone informed of the latest developments
For the pot	For food or cooking
The pot calling the kettle black	Someone making criticisms about someone else which could equally well apply to themselves
Take pot luck	Take a chance that whatever is available will prove to be good or acceptable

Sell something for a mess of pottage	Sell something for a ridiculously small amount
A pound to a penny	It is extremely likely
Pour your heart out	Express your deepest feelings or thoughts in a full and unrestrained way
Pour oil on troubled waters	Try to settle a disagreement or dispute with words intended to placate or pacify those involved
Keep your powder dry	Be ready for action; remain alert for a possible emergency
Do someone or something a power of good	Be very beneficial to someone or something
Practice makes perfect	Regular exercise of an activity or skill is the way to become proficient in it
Not have a prayer	Have no chance at all of succeeding at something
Make your presence felt	Have a strong and obvious effect on others or on a situation
Press (the) flesh	Greet people by shaking hands (of a celebrity or politician)
A pretty penny	A large sum of money
Sitting pretty	In an advantageous position or situation
Everyone has their price	Everyone can be won over by money

A price on someone's head	A reward offered for someone's capture or death
Price yourself out of the market	Be unable to compete commercially
What price - ?	Used to ask what has become of something or to suggest that something has or would become worthless
Pride goes (or comes) before a fall	If you're too conceited or self-important, something will happen to make you look foolish
Prime the pump	Stimulate or support the growth or success of something, especially by supplying it with money
The primrose path	The pursuit of pleasure, especially when it is seen to bring disastrous consequences
Prisoner of conscience	A person detained or imprisoned because of their religious or political beliefs
Take no prisoners	Be ruthlessly aggressive or uncompromising in the pursuit of your objectives
The pros and cons	The arguments for and against something; the advantages and disadvantages of something
Prodigal son	A person who leaves home to lead a spendthrift and extravagant way of life but later makes a repentant return

The oldest profession	A practice of working as a prostitute
Keep (or maintain) a low profile	Avoid attracting public notice or comment
Prolong the agony	Cause a difficult or unpleasant situation to last longer than necessary
The proof of the pudding is in the eating	The real value of something can be judged only from practical experience or results and not from appearance or theory
Under protest	After expressing your objection or reluctance; unwillingly
Prunes and prisms	Used to denote a prim and affected speech, look or manner
Go public	Become a public company
In the public eye	The state of being known or of interest to people in general, especially through the media
Like pulling teeth	Extremely difficult or laborious to do
Pull the plug	Prevent something from happening or continuing; put a stop to something
Pull strings	Make use of your influence and contacts to gain an advantage unofficially or unfairly
Pull together	Cooperate in a task or undertaking
Feel (or take) the pulse of	Ascertain the general mood or opinion of

Beat someone to the punch	Anticipate or forestall someone's actions
Sell someone a pup	Swindle someone, especially by selling them something that is worthless
In purdah	In seclusion
Pure and simple	And nothing else
Pure as the driven snow	Completely pure
Born in (or to) the purple	Born into a reigning family or privileged class
A purple patch	An ornate or elaborate passage in a literary composition
Push your luck	Act rashly or presumptuously on the assumption that you will continue to be successful or in favour
Quantum leap	A sudden large increase or advance
Queen Anne's dead	Used humorously or ironically to suggest that a piece of supposed 'news' is in fact stale
The Queensberry Rules	Standard rules of polite or acceptable behaviour
No question asked	Without any enquiries being made, especially ones thought likely to produce incriminating or embarrassing results
Cut someone to the quick	Cause someone deep distress by a hurtful remark or action

Be quids in	Be in a position where you have profited or are likely to profit from something
Call it quits	Decide to abandon an activity or venture, especially so as to cut your losses
On the qui vive	On the alert or lookout
Quote-unquote	Used parenthetically when speaking to indicate the beginning and end (or just the beginning) of a statement or passage that you are repeating, especially to emphasize the speaker's detachment from or disagreement with the original
The three Rs	Reading, (w)riting, and (a)rithmetic, regard as the fundamentals of elementary education
Breed like rabbits	Reproduce prolifically
Buy the rabbit	Fare badly; come off worse
Pull (or bring) a rabbit out of the (or a) hat	Used to describe an action that is fortuitous, and may involve sleight of hand or deception
A race against time	A situation in which someone attempts to do or complete something before a particular time or before something else happens
At rack and manger	Amid abundance or plenty

Go to rack and ruin	Gradually deteriorate in condition because of neglect; fall into disrepair
Rack your brains (or brain)	Make a great effort to think of or remember something
Rags to riches (from)	Used to describe a person's rise from a state of extreme poverty to one of great wealth
All the rage	Very popular or fashionable
At the end of the rainbow	Used to refer to something much sought after but impossible to attain
Take a rain check	Said when politely refusing an offer, with the implication that you may take it up at a later date
A rainy day	A possible time of need, usually financial need, in the future
Raise a dust	Cause turmoil
Raise your hat to someone	Admire or applaud someone
Raise the roof	Make or cause someone to make a lot of noise inside a building, for example through cheering
Rake over (old) coals (or rake over the ashes)	Revive the memory of a past event which is best forgotten
A rake's progress	A progressive deterioration, especially through self indulgence
Thin as a rake	Very thin (of a person or animal)

Hold someone or something to ransom	Hold someone prisoner and demand payment for their release
Rap someone on (or over) the knuckles	Rebuke or criticize someone
Take the rap	Be punished or blamed, especially for something that is not your fault or for which others are equally responsible
Rare bird	An exceptional person or thing; a rarity
Raring to go	Very keen and eager to make a start
Rats deserting a sinking ship	People hurrying to get away from an enterprise or organization that is failing
Rattle someone's cage	Make someone feel angry or annoyed, usually deliberately
Touch someone on the raw	Upset someone by referring to a subject about which they are extremely sensitive
Ray of sunshine	Someone or something that brings happiness into the lives of others
Read between the lines	Look for or discover a meaning that is hidden or implied rather than explicitly stated
Read someone like a book	Be able to understand someone's thoughts and motives clearly or easily

A red herring	Something, especially a clue, which is or is intended to be misleading or distracting
Red in tooth and claw	Involving savage or merciless conflict or competition
A red letter day	A pleasantly memorable, fortunate, or happy day
A broken reed	A weak or ineffectual person, especially one on whose support it is foolish to rely
In the last resort	Whatever else happens or is the case; ultimately
Give it a rest	Used to ask someone to stop doing or talking about something that the speaker finds irritating or tedious
Revenge is a dish best served (or eaten) cold	Vengeance is often more satisfying if it is not exacted immediately
Rhyme or reason	Logical explanation or reason
Cut a (or the) ribbon	Perform an opening ceremony, usually by formally cutting a ribbon strung across the entrance to a building, road, etc.
For the ride	For pleasure or interest, rather than any serious purpose
Ride off into the sunset	Achieve a happy conclusion to something

Rob Peter to pay Paul	Take something away from one person to pay another, leaving the former at a disadvantage; discharge one debt only to incur another
Get your rocks off	Obtain pleasure or satisfaction
The new rock and roll	Something that is (temporarily) highly fashionable
On the rocks	Experiencing difficulties and likely to fail (of a relationship or enterprise)
Off your rocker	Crazy
Not rocket science	Used to indicate that something is not very difficult to understand
Rise like a rocket (and fall like a stick)	Rise suddenly and dramatically (and subsequently fall in a similar manner)
Rocking-horse manure	Something extremely rare
Make a rod for your own back	Do something likely to cause difficulties for yourself later
A rod in pickle	A punishment in store
On a roll	Experiencing a prolonged spell of success or good luck
Roll up your sleeves	Prepare to fight or work
Strike someone off the rolls (or roll)	Debar a solicitor from practicing after dishonesty or other misconduct

A roller-coaster ride	An experience in which circumstances change rapidly and in a volatile manner from one extreme to another
Be rolling (in it or in money)	Be very rich
A rolling stone	A person who does not settle in one place for long
Rolling drunk	So drunk as to be swaying or staggering
A Roman holiday	An occasion on which enjoyment or profit is derived from the suffering or discomfort of others
All roads lead to Rome	There are many different ways of reaching the same goal or conclusion
Rome was not built in a day	A complex or ambitious task is bound to take a long time and should not be rushed
When in Rome (do as the Romans do)	When abroad or in an unfamiliar environment you should adopt the customs or behaviour of those around you
Go through (or hit) the roof	Reach extreme or unexpected height; become exorbitant (of prices or figures)
A roof over your head	A place in which you can stay and find shelter
Shout something from the rooftops	Talk about something openly and jubilantly, especially something previously kept secret

No (or not) room to swing a cat	Used in reference to a very confined space
Room at the top	Opportunity to join an elite or the top ranks of a profession
Put down roots	Begin to lead a settled life in a particular place
Root and branch	Used to express thorough or radical nature of a process or operation
Give someone enough rope (or plenty of rope)	Give a person enough freedom of action to bring about their own downfall
On the ropes	In a desperate position; in a state of near collapse or defeat
No rose without a thorn	Every apparently desirable situation has its share of trouble or difficulty
Not all roses	Not entirely perfect or agreeable
Under the rose	In confidence; under pledge of secrecy
The rot sets in	A rapid succession of (usually unaccountable) failures begins
Rough and ready	Rough or crude but effective
Rough and tumble	A situation without rules or organization; a free-for-all
Rough around the edges	Having a few imperfections
A rough diamond	A person who has genuinely fine qualities but uncouth manners

Rough edges	Slight imperfections in someone or something that is basically satisfactory
Ride roughshod over	Carry out your own plans or wishes with arrogant disregard for others
The last roundup	Death
A roving eye	A tendency to flirt or be constantly looking to start a new sexual relationship
Royal road to	A way of attaining or reaching something without trouble
Rub of the green	The influence of luck, seen as being advantageous or more usually disadvantageous
Rub our hands	Show keen satisfaction or expectation
Rub someone's nose in something (or rub it in)	Emphatically or repeatedly draw someone's attention to an embarrassing or painful fact
Rub shoulders	Associate or come into contact with another person
Rub someone (up) the wrong way	Irritate or repel someone
Burn rubber	Drive very quickly
Rubber cheque	A cheque that is returned unpaid
Cross the Rubicon	Take an irrevocable step

A rude awakening	A sudden realization of the true (bad) state of affairs, having previously been under the illusion that everything was satisfactory
Ruffle someone's feathers	Cause someone to become annoyed or upset
Smooth someone's ruffled feathers	Make someone less angry or irritated by using soothing words
Rule of thumb	A broadly accurate guide or principle, based on experience or practice rather than theory
Rule the roost	Be in complete control
Rumour has it	It is rumoured
Give someone or something a (good) run for their money	Provide someone or something with challenging competition or opposition
Have a (good) run for your money	Derive reward or enjoyment in return for your outlay or efforts
Run foul of	Come into conflict with; go against
Run high	Be strong or tumultuous
Run into the sand	Come to nothing
Run of the mill	The ordinary or undistinguished type
Run someone out of town	Force someone to leave a place

Give someone the runaround	Deceive and confuse someone; avoid answering someone's question directly
Do a runner	Leave hastily, especially to avoid paying for something or. to escape from somewhere
A running battle	A confrontation that has gone on for a long time
Rush your fences	Act with undue haste
A rush of blood (to the head)	A sudden attack of wild irrationality in your thinking or actions
In a rut	Follow a fixed (especially tedious or dreary) pattern of behaviour that is difficult to change
A Sabbath day's journey	A short and easy journey
Hold the sack	Bear an unwelcome responsibility
In sackcloth and ashes	Manifesting grief or repentance
There's safety in number	Being in a group of people makes you feel more confident or secure about taking action
Put salt on the tail of	Capture
Rub salt into the (or someone's) wound	Make a painful experience even more painful for someone
The salt of the earth	A person or group of people of great kindness, reliability, or honesty

Sit below the salt	Be of lower social standing or worth
Take something with a pinch (or grain) of salt	Regard something as exaggerated; believe only part of something
Worth your salt	Good or competent at the job or profession specified
Good Samaritan	A charitable or helpful person
The sands (of time) are running out	The allotted time is nearly at an end
Packed like sardines	Crowded very close together
What's sauce for the goose is sauce for the gander	What is appropriate in one case is also appropriate in the other case in question
Go without saying	Too well known or obvious to need to be mentioned
Throw away the scabbard	Abandon all thought of making peace
Like a scalded cat	At a very fast speed
The scales fall from someone's eyes	Someone is no longer deceived
Make yourself scarce	Surreptitiously disappear; keep out of the way
Scarlet woman	A notoriously promiscuous or immoral woman

Behind the scenes	In private; secretly
Change of scene (or scenery)	A move to different surroundings
The scheme of things	The organization of things in general; the way the world is
Scoop the pool (or the kitty)	Be completely successful; gain everything
From scratch	From the very beginning, especially without utilizing or relying on any previous work for assistance
Have a screw loose	Be slightly eccentric or mentally disturbed
At sea (all)	Confused or unable to decide what to do
Bursting (or bulging) at the seams	Full to overflowing (of a place or building)
On second thoughts	Having reconsidered a matter (and arrived at a different opinion or decision)
Second nature	A characteristic or habit in someone that appears to be instinctive because that person has behaved in a particular way so often
Seize the day	Make the most of the present moment
In (or into) the shade	In (or into) a position of relative inferiority or obscurity

Shades of	Used to suggest reminiscence of or comparison with someone or something specified
Afraid of (or frightened of) your own shadow	Unreasonably timid or nervous
On Shank's pony	Using your own legs as a means of transport
Lick (or knock or whip) someone or something into shape	Act forcefully to bring someone or something into a fitter, more efficient, or better-organized state
The shape of things to come	The way the future is likely to develop
Sharp as a needle	Extremely quick-witted
Count sheep	Count imaginary sheep jumping over a fence one by one in an attempt to send yourself to sleep
Make sheep's eyes at someone	Look at someone in a foolishly amorous way
Separate the sheep from the goats	Divide people or things into superior and inferior groups
Off the shelf	Not designed or made to order but taken form existing stock or supplies
Make shift	Do what you want to do in spite of not having ideal conditions; get along somehow

Another pair of shoes	Quite a different matter or state of things
Dead men's shoes	Property or a position coveted by a prospective successor but available only on a person's death
Where the shoe pinches	Where your difficulty or trouble is
On a shoestring	On a small or inadequate budget
Shoot the breezes (or the bull)	Have a casual conversation
Shoot your cuffs	Pull your shirt cuffs out to project beyond the cuffs of your jacket or coat
Shoot someone or something down in flames	Forcefully destroy an argument or proposal
Shoot from the hip	React suddenly or without careful consideration of your words or actions
Shoot a line	Describe something in an exaggerated, untruthful, or boastful way
Shoot yourself in the foot	Inadvertently make a situation worse for yourself; demonstrate gross incompetence
In short order	Immediately; rapidly
The short end of the stick	The disadvantage in a situation; a bad deal
Be on someone's shoulder	Keep a close check on someone

Look over your shoulder	Be anxious or insecure about a possible danger
A shoulder to cry on	Someone who listens sympathetically to another person's problems
Shout the odds	Talk loudly and in an opinionated way
Show your hand (or cards)	Disclose your plans
Show a leg	Get out of bed; get up
Send someone to the showers	Fail early on in a race or contest
A thing of shreds and patches	Something made up of scraps of fabric patched together
Short shrift	Rapid and unsympathetic dismissal; curt treatment
Shrinking violet	An exaggeratedly shy person
Sick and tired	Annoyed about or bored with something and unwilling to put up with it any longer
Sick as a parrot	Extremely disappointed
Sick to death	Very annoyed by something and unwilling to put up with it any longer
Let the side down	Fail to meet the expectations of your colleagues or friends, especially by mismanaging something
On the side	Rather
On (or from) the sidelines	In (or from) a position where you are observing a situation but are unable or unwilling to be directly involved in it

Out of sight	Extremely good; excellent (often used as an exclamation)
Out of sight, out of mind	You soon forget people or things that are no longer visible or present
Raise (or lower) your sights	Become more (or less) ambitious; increase (or lower) your expectations
A sight for sore eyes	A person or thing that is very attractive or that you are extremely pleased or relieved to see
Sign your own death warrant	Do something that ensures your own demise or downfall
Silence is golden	It's often wise to say nothing
The silent majority	The majority of people, regarded as holding moderate opinions but rarely expressing them
Make a silk purse out of a sow's ear	Turn something inferior into something of top quality
Be born with a silver spoon in your mouth	Be born into a wealthy family of high social standing
Have a silver tongue	Be eloquent or persuasive
On a silver platter (or salver)	Without having been asked or sought for; without requiring any effort or return from the recipient
A silver lining	A positive or more hopeful aspect to a bad situation, even though this may not be immediately apparent

The silver screen	The cinema industry; cinema films collectively
For your sins	Used to suggest that a task or duty is so onerous or unpleasant that it must be a punishment
Sing a different tune (or song)	Change your opinion about or attitude towards someone or something
A (or that) sinking feeling	An unpleasant feeling caused by the realization that something unpleasant or undesirable has happened or is about to happen
Siren song (or call)	The appeal of something that is also considered to be harmful or dangerous
Sit (heavy) on the stomach	Take a long time to be digested (of food)
Sitting duck	A person or thing with no protection against an attack or other source of danger
At sixes and sevens	In a state or total confusion or dis-array
Six feet under	Dead and buried
On a sixpence	Within a small area or short distance (of a stop or turn)
A skeleton in the cupboard	A discreditable or embarrassing fact that someone wishes to keep secret
Under the skin	In reality, as opposed to superficial appearances

The sky is the limit	There is practically no limit
Cut someone some slack	Allow someone some leeway; make allowances for someone's behaviour
Slap and tickle	Physical amorous play
Slap on the wrist	A mild reprimand or punishment
Put something to sleep	Kill (an animal, especially an old, sick, or badly injured one) painlessly
Sleep with one eye open	Sleep very lightly so as to be aware of what is happening around you
Let sleeping dogs lie	Avoid interfering in a situation that is currently causing no problems, but may well do so as a consequence of such interference
Take someone for a sleigh ride	Mislead someone
Let something slide	Negligently allow something to deteriorate
Give someone the slip	Evade or escape from someone
Slip of the pen (or the tongue)	A minor mistake in writing (or speech)
Slip on a banana skin	Make a silly and embarrassing mistake
Have a smack at	Make an attempt at or attack on
The (wee) small hours	The early hours of the morning immediately after midnight

Small is beautiful	The belief that something small-scale is better than a large-scale equivalent
Small beer	Something trivial or insignificant
Small potatoes	Something insignificant or unimportant
Small print	Inconspicuous details or conditions printed in an agreement or contract, especially ones that may prove unfavourable
Smart alec (or aleck)	A person considered irritating because they know a great deal or always have a clever answer to a question
Smell of the lamp	Show signs of laborious study and effort
Come up (or out) smelling of roses (or violets)	Make a lucky escape from a difficult situation with your reputation intact
Watch someone's smoke	Observe another person's activity
A smoking gun (or pistol)	A piece of incontrovertible evidence
A snake in the grass	A treacherous or deceitful person
Make it snappy	Be quick about it
No soap	No chance of something happening or occurring
On your soapbox	Energetically stating your opinions, especially ones which are already well known on a subject that you often revert to

Knock (or blow) someone's socks off	Amaze or impress someone
Pull your socks up	Make an effort to improve your work, performance, or behaviour
Have a soft spot for	Be fond of or affectionate towards
Soft soap	Persuasive flattery
Thirty-something (or forty-something, etc.)	An unspecified age between thirty and forty
Son of a gun	A humorous or affectionate way of addressing or referring to someone
For a song	Very cheaply
On song	Performing well; in good form
A song in your heart	A feeling of great or euphoric happiness
A sop to Cerberus	Something offered to appease someone
Sorcerer's apprentice	A person who having instigated a process is unable to control it
More in sorrow than in anger	With regret or sadness rather than with anger
Head south	Deteriorate
Have the right sow by the ear	Have the correct understanding of a situation
Sow the seed (or seeds) of	Do something which will eventually bring about a particular result

Call a spade a spade	Speak plainly or bluntly, without avoiding issues which are unpleasant or embarrassing
It speaks well for	Something places someone or something in a favourable light
Speak for yourself	Give your own opinions
Speak in tongues	Speak in an unknown language during religious worship
Speak your mind	Express your feelings or opinions frankly
On spec	In the hope of success but without any specific plan or instructions
Spill the beans	Reveal secret information, especially unintentionally or indiscreetly
The spirit is willing (but the flesh is weak)	Someone has good intentions (but yields to temptation and fails to live up to them)
The spirit moves someone	Someone feels inclined to do something
Spit and polish	Extreme neatness or smartness
Spit it out	Used to urge someone to say, confess, or divulge something quickly,
Make a splash	Attract a great deal of attention
Split the vote	Attract votes from another candidate or party with the result that both are defeated by a third (of a candidate or minority party)

Put a spoke in someone's wheel	Prevent someone from carrying out a plan
Win the wooden spoon	Be the least successful contestant; win the booby prize
Put someone on the spot	Force someone into a situation in which they must make a difficult decision or answer a difficult question
Square the circle	Do something that is considered to be impossible
Squeaky clean	Beyond reproach; without vice
A stab in the back	A treacherous act or statement; a betrayal
Hold the stage	Dominate a scene of action or forum of debate
Go to the stake for	Do anything to defend a specified belief, opinion, or person
Leave someone or something standing	Be much better or faster than someone or something else (of a person or thing)
Have stares in your eyes	Be idealistically hopeful or enthusiastic, especially about a possible future in entertainment or sport
Reach for the stars	Have high or ambitious aims
Someone's star is rising	Someone is becoming ever more successful or popular

Take the starch out of someone	Shake someone's confidence, especially by humiliating them
State of the art	The most recent stage in the development of a product, incorporating the newest ideas and the most up-to-date features
State of grace	A condition of being free from sin
Steal someone's clothes	Appropriate someone's ideas or policies
Steal a march on	Gain an advantage over someone, typically by acting before they do
Steal someone's thunder	Win praise for yourself by pre-empting someone else's attempt to impress
Have steam coming out of your ears	Be extremely angry or irritated
Be made of sterner stuff	Have a stronger character and be more able to overcome problems than others (of a person)
Stick it to someone	Treat someone harshly or severely
Stick your neck out	Risk incurring criticism, anger, or danger by acting or speaking boldly
Stick to someone's fingers	Be embezzled by a person (of money)
A stiff upper lip	A quality of uncomplaining stoicism
Still waters run deep	A quiet or placid manner may conceal a passionate nature

A stitch in time	If you sort out a problem immediately, it may save a lot of extra work later
On the stocks	In construction or preparation
Take stock	Review or make an assessment of a particular situation
An army marches on its stomach	Soldiers or workers can only fight or function effectively if they have been well fed
On a full (or an empty) stomach	Having (or without having) eaten beforehand
Cast (or throw) the first stone	Be the first to accuse or criticize
Leave no stone unturned	Try every possible course of action in order to achieve something
A stone's throw	A short distance
Fall on stony ground	Be ignored or badly received (of words or a suggestion)
Fall between two stools	Fail to be or take one of two satisfactory alternatives
Pull out all the stops	Make a very great effort; go to elaborate lengths
Stop someone's mouth	Bribe or otherwise induce a person to keep silent abot something
Put a (or the) stopper on	Cause something to end or become quiet
The lull (or calm) before the storm	A period of unusual tranquility or stability that seems likely to presage difficult time

A storm in a teacup	Great excitement or anger about a trivial matter
It's (or that's) the story of my life	Used to lament the fact that a particular misfortune has happened too often in your experience
Go straight	Live an honest life after being a criminal
Clutch (or grasp or catch) at straws	Do, say, or believe anything, however unlikely or inadequate, which seems to offer hope in a desperate situation
The last (or final) straw	A further difficulty or annoyance, typically minr in itself but coming on top of a whole series of difficulties, that makes a situation unbearable
Up (or right up) your street	Well suited to your tastes, interests, or abilities
Go from strength to strength	Develop or progress with increasing success
A tower (or pillar) of strength	A person who can be relied upon to be a source of strong support and comfort
Stricken in years	Used euphemistically to describe someone old and feeble
Take something in your stride	Deal with something difficult or unpleasant in a calm and competent way
Strike oil	Attain prosperity or success
Strike while the iron is hot	Makes use of an opportunity immediately

Have a second string to your bow	Have an alternative resource that you can make use of if the first one fails
Do your stuff	Perform a task at which you are particularly skilled or which is in your particular area of expertise
Nothing succeeds like success	Success leads to opportunities for further and greater successes
Suck someone dry	Exhaust someone's physical, material, or emotional resources
Of a sudden (all)	Suddenly
Sunny side up	Fried on one side only (of an egg)
Sure as eggs is eggs (also sure as fate)	Without any doubt; absolutely certain
Sure thing	Certainly; of course
Surf the net	Move from site to site on the internet
Survival of the fittest	The continued existence of organisms which are best adapted to their environment, with the extinction of others, as a concept in the Darwinian theory of evolution
One swallow doesn't make a summer	A single fortunate event does not mean that what follows will also be good
Swear black is white	Vigorously maintain anything, however unlikely, in order to get what you want

Pick up the tab	Pay for something
Lay something on the table	Make something known so hat is can be freely and sensible discussed
Turn the tables	Reverse your position relative to someone else, especially by turning a position of disadvantage into one of advantage
Under the table	Drunk to the point of unconsciousness
A piece of old tackie	An easy task
Tread tackie	Drive or accelerate
The tail wags the dog	The less important or subsidiary factor or thing dominates a situation; the usual roles are reversed
With your tail between your legs	In state of dejection or humiliation
Take it or leave it	Said to convey that the offer you have made is not negotiable and that you are indifferent to another's reaction to it
For the taking	Ready or available for someone to take advantage of (of a person or thing)
Talk a good game	Talk convincingly yet fail to act effectively
Talk the hind leg off a donkey	Talk incessantly

A tall poppy	A privileged or distinguished person
In tandem	One behind another
A tangled web	A complex, difficult, and confusing situation or thing
It takes two to tango	Both parities involved in a situation or argument are equally responsible for it
On tap	Freely available whenever needed
Have (or get) someone or something taped	Understand someone or something fully
On the tapis	Under consideration or discussion (of a subject)
Beat (or whale) the tar out of	Beat or thrash severely
Tar and feather	Smear with tar and then cover with feathers as a punishment
Tar people with the same brush	Consider specified people to have the same faults
Take someone to task	Reprimand or criticize someone severely for a fault or mistake
Go for your tea	Be murdered
Not for all the tea in China	Not at any price; certainly not!
Tea and sympathy	Hospitality and consolation offered to a distressed person

Tell it like it is	Describe the true facts of a situation no matter how unpleasant they may be
Tell me another	Used as an expression of disbelief or incredulity
Tell tales (out of school)	Gossip about or reveal another person's wrongdoing or faults
Tell someone where to get off (or where they get off)	Angrily rebuke someone
Tell someone where to put (or what to do with) something	Angrily or emphatically reject something
There's no telling	It is impossible to know what has happened or will happen
You're telling me!	Used to emphasize that you are already well aware of something or in complete agreement with a statement
Tempt fate (or providence)	Act rashly
Ten out of ten	Full marks (used to congratulate someone for doing something perfectly)
On tenterhooks	In a state of suspense or agitation because of uncertainty about a future event

Come to terms with	Come to accept a new and painful or difficult event or situation
Terminate someone with extreme prejudice	Murder or assassinate someone
Go (or come) with the territory	Be an unavoidable result of a particular situation
Test the water	Judge people's feelings or opinions before taking further action
Thank your lucky stars	Feel grateful for your good fortune
No thanks to	Not because of; despite
Thanks for the buggy ride	Used as a way of thanking someone for their help
Thanks for nothing	Used ironically to indicate that what someone has done or said is extremely unwelcome to you
And all that (or and that)	And that sort of thing; and so in
That's that	There is nothing more to do or say about the matter
Been there, done that	Used to express past experience of or familiarity with something
Be there for someone	Be available to provide support or comfort for someone, especially at a time of adversity
A bit thick	More than you can tolerate; unfair or unreasonable

Give someone (or get) a thick ear	Punish someone (or be punished) with a blow, especially on the ear
Thick and fast	Rapidly and in great numbers
Thick as thieves	Very close or friendly; sharing secrets (of two or more people)
Through thick and thin	Under all circumstances, no matter how difficult
Have a thin time	Have a wretched or uncomfortable time
The thin end of the wedge	An action or procedure of little importance in itself, but which is likely to lead to more serious development
The thin end of the wedge	An action or procedure of little importance in itself, but which is likely to lead to more serious developments
Be on to a good thing	Have found a job or other situation that is pleasant, profitable, or easy
A close (or near) thing	A narrow avoidance of something unpleasant
Do the in-thing	Engage in the particular form of behaviour typically associated with someone or something
Do your own thing	Follow your own interests or inclinations regardless of others
Hear (or see) things	Imagine that your can hear (or see) something that is not in fact there

One of those things	Used to indicate that you wish to pass over an unfortunate event or experience by regarding it as unavoidable or to be accepted
Tell (or teach) someone a thing or two	Impart useful information or experience
Things that go bump in the night	Ghosts; supernatural beings
Have (got) another think coming	Used to express the speaker's disagreement with or unwillingness to do something suggested by someone else
Think nothing of it	Do not apologize or feel bound to show gratitude (used as a polite respose)
Think on your feet	React to events quickly and effectively
Think twice	Consider a course of action carefully before embarking on it
Put on your thinking cap	Meditate on a problem
Third time lucky	After twice failing to accomplish something, the third attempt may be successful
A thorn in someone's side (or flesh)	A source of continual annoyance or trouble

Hang by a thread	Be in highly precarious state
Lose the (or your) thread	Be unable to follow what someone is saying or remember what you are going to say next
Three musketeers	Three close associates or inseparable friends
Threescore and ten	The age of seventy
Thrills and spills	The excitement of dangerous sports or entertainments, especially as experienced by spectators
Be at each other's throats	Quarrel or fight persistently (of people or organizations)
Cut your own throat	Bring about your own downfall by your actions
On the tiles	Away from home having a wild or enjoyable time and not returning until late in the evening or early in the morning
Have (or with) your fingers (or hand) in the till	Stealing from your employer
Full tilt (at)	With maximum energy or force; at top speed
Tilt at windmills	Attack imaginary enemies or evils
For the time being	For the present; until some other arrangement is made

Give someone the time of day	Be pleasantly polite or friendly to someone
In your own time	At a time and a rate decided by yourself
Not before time	Used to convey that something now happening or about to happen should have happened earlier
Once upon a time	At some time in the past (used as a conventional opening of a story).
Pass the time of day	Exchange a greeting or casual remarks
The time of your life	A period or occasion of exceptional enjoyment
Time is money	Time is a valuable resource, therefore it's better to do things as quickly as possible
Time was	There was a time
Time will tell	The truth or correctness of something will only be established at some time in the future
Not give (or care) a tinker's curse (damn)	Not care at all
Be on the tip of your tongue	Be almost but not quite able to bring a particular word or name to mind
Tip your hand (or mitt)	Reveal your intentions inadvertently
Tip your hat (or cap)	Raise or touch your hat or cap as a way of greeting or acknowledge someone

Tip (or turn) the scales (or balance)	Be the deciding factor; make the critical difference (of a circumstance or event)
Tip someone the wink	Give someone private information; secretly warn someone of something
Tired and emotional	Drunk
Be toast	Be or be likely to become finished, defunct, or dead
Have someone on toast	Be in a position to deal with someone as you wish
On your tod	On your own; alone
Make someone's toes curl	Bring about an extreme reaction in someone, either of pleasure or disgust
On your toes	Ready for any eventuality
A toe in the door	A (first) chance of ultimately achieving what you want; a position from which further progress is possible
Toe the line	Accept the authority, principles, or policies of a particular group, especially under pressure
Turn up your toes	Die
Not able to do something for toffee	Be totally incompetent at doing something
Set tongues wagging	Be the cause of much gossip or rumour

Someone's tongue is hanging out	Someone is very eager for something, especially a drink
Tongue in cheek (with)	Speaking or writing in an ironic or insincere way
Fight tooth and nail	Fight very fiercely
From top to bottom	Completely; thoroughly
On top of the world	Happy and elated
Over the top	To an excessive or exaggerated degree, in particular so as to go beyond reasonable or acceptable limits
Top and tail	Remove the top and bottom of a fruit or vegetable while preparing it as food
Top dollar	A very high price
Carry a torch for	Feel (especially unrequited) love for
Hand on (or pass) the torch	Pass on a tradition, especially one of learning or enlightenment
Put to the torch (or put a torch to)	Destroy by burning
Not give (or care) a toss	Not care at all
A soft (or easy) touch	Someone who is easily manipulated; a person or task easily handled

Touch and go	Possible but very uncertain (of an outcome, especially one that is desired)
Touch bottom	Be at the lowest or worst point
Tough as old boots	Very sturdy or resilient
Tough it out	Endure a period of difficult conditions
Go to town	Do something thoroughly or extravagantly, with a great deal of energy and enthusiasm
On the town	Enjoying the entertainments, especially the nightlife, of a city or town
Town and gown	Non-members and members of a university in a particular place
Throw your toys out of the pram	Have a temper tantrum
Make tracks (for)	Leave (for a place)
The wrong side of the tracks	A poor or less prestigious part of town
As much as the traffic will bear	As much as the trade or market will tolerate; as much as is economically viable
Shut your trap	Be silent; stop talking
A treat	Used to indicate that someone or something does something specified very well or satisfactorily

Out of your tree	Completely stupid, mad
Up a tree	In a difficult situation without escape; cornered
Trial and error	The process of experimenting with various methods of doing something until you find the most successful
Trial by television (or the media)	Discussion of a case or controversy on television or in the media involving or implying accusations against a particular person
In a trice	In a moment; very quickly
Do the trick	Achieve the required result
Every trick in the book	Every available method of achieving what you want
The oldest trick in the book	A ruse so hackneyed that it should no longer deceive anyone
A trick worth two of that	A much better plan or expedient
Tricks of the trade	Special ingenious techniques used in a profession or craft, especially those that are little known by outsiders
Tried and true	Proved effective or reliable by experience
In trim	Slim and healthy
Trim your sails	Make changes to suit your new circumstances
Trip the light fantastic	Dance
Right as a trivet	Perfectly all right; in good health

Work like a Trojan	Work extremely hard
A Trojan horse	A programme designed to breach the security of a computer system, especially by ostensibly program, in order to erase, corrupt, or remove data
Off your trolley	Crazy
Get someone into trouble	Make (an unmarried woman) pregnant
Keep on trucking	Used as an encouragement to keep going, not to give up
Blow your own trumpet	Talk openly and boastfully about your achievements
A turn-up for the book	A completely unexpected event or occurrence; a surprise
Turn turtle	Turn upside down
Never the twain shall meet	Two people or things are too different to exist alongside or understand each other
Twenty-four seven	All the time; twenty-four hours a day, seven days a week
Twiddle your thumbs	So bored or idle because you have nothing to do
A twinkle in someone's eye	Something that is still in the pre-planning stage and on which no action has yet been taken, especially a child not as yet conceived
Two-way street	A situation or relationship between two people or groups in which action is required from both parties; something that works both ways

Weather the storm	Survive a period of difficulty
Be a weight off your mind	Comes as a great relief after you have been worried
Be worth your (or its) weight in gold	Be extremely useful or helpful
Wet the baby's head	Celebrate a baby's birth with a drink, usually an alcoholic one
Wet behind the ears	Lacking experience; immature
A wet blanket	Someone who has a depressing or discouraging effect on others
Wheel and deal	Engage in commercial or political scheming
Blow the whistle on	Bring an illicit activity to and end by informing on the person responsible
Whistle in the wind	Try unsuccessfully to influence something that cannot be changed
Show the white feather	Appear cowardly
A white elephant	A possession that is useless or troublesome, especially one that is expensive to maintain or difficult to dispose of
White hope	A person expected to bring much success to a team or organization
A white knight	A company that makes a welcome bid for a company facing an unwelcome takeover bid

The whys and wherefores	The reasons for or details of something
A wild goose chase	A foolish and hopeless search for or pursuit of something unattainable
Where there's a will there's a way	Determination will overcome any obstacle
Win (or earn) your spurs	Gain your first distinction or honours
Between wind and water	At a vulnerable point
Gone with the wind	Gone completely; having disappeared without trace
Take the wind out of someone's sails	Frustrate a person by unexpectedly anticipating an action or remark
Go out (of) the window	No longer exist; disappear (of a plan or pattern of behaviour)
New wine in old bottles	Something new or innovatory added to an existing or established system or organization
In the wings	Ready to do something or to be used at the appropriate time
If wishes were horses, beggars would ride	If you could achieve your aims simply by wishing for them, life would be very easy
The wish is father to the thought	We believe a thing because we wish it to be true

Be at your wits' end	Be overwhelmed with difficulties and at a loss as to what to do next
Pit your wits against	Complete with someone or something
The witching hour	Midnight
Cry wolf	Call for help when it is not needed; raise a false alarm
Keep the wolf from the door	Have enough money to avert hunger or starvation
Throw someone to the wolves	Leave someone to be roughly treated or criticized without typing to help or defend them
Cannot see the wood for the trees	Fail to grasp the main issue because of over-attention to details
Touch wood	Said in order to prevent a confident statement from bringing bad luck
Vanish into (or come or crawl out of) the woodwork	Disappear into (or emerge from) obscurity
Give someone the works	Treat someone harshly
A bad workman blames his tools	Someone who has done something badly will seek to lay the blame on the equipment rather than admit to their own lack of skill
The best of both (or all possible) worlds	The benefits of widely differing situations, enjoyed at the same time

A man (or woman) of the world	A person who is experienced and practical in human affairs
The world, the flesh, and the devil	All forms of temptation to sin
The world is your oyster	You are in a position to take the opportunities that life has to offer
A worm's-eye view	The view looking up at something from ground level
Not to worry	Used to reassure someone by telling them that a situation is not serious
So much the worse for	Used to suggest that a problem, failure, or other unfortunate event or situation is the fault of a person specified and that the speaker does not fell any great concern about it
Wring someone's withers	Stir someone's emotions or conscience
The writing is on the wall	There are clear signs that something unpleasant or unwelcome is going to happen
Spin a yarn	Tell a story, especially a long and complicated one

Printed in Great Britain
by Amazon

73975643R10130